BRITAIN'S
TOP TOURIST
ATTRACTIONS

JOSEPH FULLMAN

Navigator Guides Ltd
The Old Post Office, Swanton Novers
Melton Constable, Norfolk NR24 2AJ
postmaster@navigatorguides.com

Copyright © Navigator Guides Ltd 2001

ISBN 1 903872-02-2

Colour reproduction by
C3 Imaging, Newcastle upon Tyne
Printed in Italy by
Printer Trento srl

CONTENTS

ALBERT DOCK

LOCATION: Liverpool, Merseyside L3
TEL: 0151 478 4499
OPENING TIMES: 10–5 daily
ADM: Adult £3, Child Free, Family £8, Conc's £1.50
GETTING THERE: Road: M62 (J5) Train: Liverpool Lime Street Station, then bus 1 or 4
FACILITIES: Large free car park, cafés, restaurants

Merseyside Maritime Museum (inc. HM Customs & Excise Museum & Museum of Liverpool Life)
FACILITIES: Café, gift shop
DISABLED: Toilets, wheelchair access
WEBSITE: www.nmgm.org.uk

Tate Gallery, Liverpool
TEL: 0151 712 7400
OPENING TIMES: 10–5.50 Tue–Sun & Bank Hol Mon
ADM: Free
FACILITIES: Gift shop, licensed restaurant
DISABLED: Wheelchair access (lift: all floors)
WEBSITE: www.tate.org.uk

Beatles Story
Tel: 0151 709 1963
OPENING TIMES: Apr–Oct: 10–6 daily, Nov–Mar: 10–5 daily
ADM: Adult £6.95, Child & Conc's £4.95, Family £17
FACILITIES: Gift shop
DISABLED: Toilets, wheelchair access
WEBSITE: www.nmgm.org.uk

NOTHING SYMBOLISES LIVERPOOL'S revitalisation better than the Albert Dock. These previously derelict 19th century brick warehouses were transformed in the 1980s into a thriving cultural complex made up of shops, cafés and restaurants alongside museums and exhibitions designed to highlight and celebrate the culture and history of the area.

At the 5-storey Merseyside Maritime Museum, you can find out about the docks themselves that were for so long the lifeblood of the city. The rigours and hardships of dockyard life are vividly recreated and there are displays on the Merchant Navy, emigration and slavery, as well as a whole gallery filled with model boats. The ground floor is given over to the HM Customs & Excise Museum, a lighthearted look at the art and practice of smuggling.

At the Museum of Liverpool Life, also housed in the same building, you can chart the rise of a distinct Liverpudlian identity through an examination of the city's music, literature and sport. The musical side of Liverpool life is further examined in the Beatles Story in the nearby Britannia Vaults, a lively tribute to the city's most famous sons using videos, dioramas and even a reconstruction of the legendary Cavern Club.

The dock's fourth great attraction, the Tate Gallery of Liverpool, is the least city-specific but is, nonetheless, an important addition to the whole, being, at present, the north of England's premier collection of modern art. Housed in an appropriately modernist-looking converted warehouse, it holds works by artists such as Damien Hirst, Andy Warhol, Francis Bacon, Lucian Freud and Henry Moore.

ALTON TOWERS

LOCATION: Alton
Staffordshire
ST10 4DB
TEL:
08705 204 060
OPENING TIMES:
April–Oct 9.30–dusk
(rides start at 10am)
ADM: Peak (w/end &
school holidays): One
day ticket: Adult £21,
Child £17, Under 4
Free; two day ticket:
Adult: £29.50, Child
£25.50, Under 4 Free,
Family £65;
Off Peak: One day
ticket: Adult £16,
Child £13, Under 4
Free; Two-day ticket:
Adult £24.50, Child
£21.50, Under 4 Free,
Family: £58
GETTING THERE:
Road: Signposted
from the M1 (J28
from the north, J23A
from the south) and
M6 (J16 from the
north, J15 from the
south)
Train: Alton, Luton &
Stafford stations
FACILITIES: On site
parking (6000
spaces), on-site
hotel, various fast
food restaurants
DISABLED:
Wheelchair access
to Park, all rides and
facilities, adapted
toilets
WEBSITE: www.
alton-towers.co.uk

Have you ever wanted to plummet 60ft into a pitch-black hole at 110mph? You have? Well, Alton Towers may just be able to help. The recent trend for Theme Parks to build larger, faster, more regurgitatingly scary rides reached its peak in the late 90s when Alton Towers unleashed "Oblivion", the world's first vertical drop rollercoaster, on an innocent public. Billed, and this is meant to be a recommendation remember, as "the ultimate in psychological and physical endurance", the ride, during the drop stage, exerts a force of 4.5G on its passengers – by way of comparison, astronauts experience a mere 3Gs on take-off.

If this doesn't leave you a gibbering wreck, fear not, there are dozens of other rides designed to test your powers of digestion to the very limit including the suspension roller-coaster 'Nemesis', 'Ripsaw', which has three 360° loops, 'Blackhole', a rollercoaster ride in total darkness, and 'Hex', the park's latest attraction, a combination of haunted house, live show and virtual reality ride

Although they're not really the reason why you're here, Alton Towers does have its more sedate attractions. Once the largest private residence in Europe, much of the house has, after a century of neglect, been restored and re-opened to the public. There are also some delightful gardens with a conservatory and Pagoda where you can wander whilst you wait for your heartbeat to come back down under 200.

@BRISTOL

LOCATION:
Harbourside, Bristol
BS1 5BD

TEL: 0117 915 5000

OPENING TIMES:
10–6 daily

ADM: Single
attraction: £6.50,
Family £19; all
attractions: £15.50,
Family £50

GETTING THERE:
Road: A4 or A38 to
Bristol and then fol-
low the brown
tourist signs
Train: Temple Meads

FACILITIES: On–site
parking, cafés,
restaurants, shops

DISABLED:
Wheelchair access
and adapted toilets

WEBSITE: www.
at-bristol.org.uk

6

Bristol has long been in the shadow of its more illustrious neighbour, Bath. While millions of tourists come every year to inspect Bath's carefully preserved history – its Roman Baths and Georgian terraces – the few that journey on to Bristol, just 12 miles away, are often disappointed by its rather nondescript modern appearance – it was heavily bombed during World War II – and lack of architectural cohesion. Now, it seems, Bristol has had enough. With the opening in summer 2000 of @Bristol, a state-of-the-art cultural complex on the redeveloped har-bourside, it appears the city has finally decid-ed to start treating its modernity as a bless-ing rather than a curse.

Everything about the project is impressive – its scale, its range of attractions, its level of ambition, its cost (some £100 million) – and its opening has given the city's self esteem a much needed shot in the arm.

Its principal attractions are Explore @Bristol, a hands-on science centre with a giant planetarium, the Orange Imaginarium, housed in a giant silver sphere reminiscent of Paris Geodé, and Wildscreen@Bristol, a natural history exhibition which contains an IMAX 3-D cinema and a walkthrough butter-fly house and botanical garden. Lavish atten-tion has been paid to the setting, with the attractions arranged around an open conti-nental-style piazza "The Millennium Square." This is lined with cafés and restaurants and decorated with numerous specially commis-sioned pieces of modern art including a walk-through fountain "The Aquarena" and a sculpture of two bronze dogs swimming in a pool of rubber.

BEAMISH

LOCATION:
Beamish, Country
Durham DH9 0RG
TEL: 01207 231 811
OPENING TIMES:
Apr–Oct 10-5 daily;
Nov–Mar (town &
tram only) 10–4
Tue–Thur & Sat–Sun
ADM:
Apr–Oct: Adult £10,
Child £6, Under 5
Free; Nov–Mar: Adult
& Child £3
GETTING THERE:
Road: A1/M1 (J23),
follow signs along
A68, A692 or A693
Bus: Service from
Durham City 10
miles south, call Go
North East 0845 606
0260
FACILITIES: On-site

BEAMISH IS ONE of the country's very best open-air museums, a 300-acre site dedicated to showing what life was like in the industrial north during the 19th and early 20th centuries. It is home to dozens and dozens of historic buildings, many of which have been transported here from sites all over the northeast and then painstakingly reassembled.

There are five sections to explore which you can travel between aboard a vintage tram: a town with streets, shops (including a pub and a grocers), and businesses – all, of course, decorated in perfect period style and inhabited by staff dressed in the costume of the times; a colliery village with a drift mine, a chapel, cottages and a school (you can take a tour of the mine and hunch along its claustrophobic 4ft-high tunnels); a Manor House with formal gardens and orchards; a farm inhabited by traditional farm animals and a railway station where you can take a ride on a full-size replica of Stephenson's Locomotive No.1 along a short length of track.

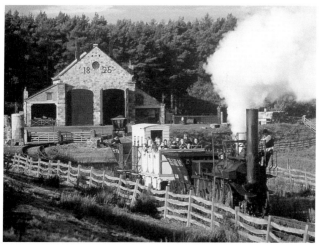

parking, cafés,
restaurant, tearoom,
gift and food shops
DISABLED:
Wheelchair access
(although site is
quite severely
sloped in places)
adapted toilets
WEBSITE: www.
beamish.org.uk

It's particularly good for children who can interact with the staff, learn old-fashioned games like hopscotch and hoops, buy sweets in the town confectioner's and (always a strangely popular choice), sit learning lessons in the Victorian school room. There's also a Victorian fairground with a hall of mirrors and a gift shop selling period souvenirs and locally-made craft produce.

BEAULIEU

LOCATION:
Beaulieu Hampshire
SO42 7ZN
TEL: 01590 612 345
OPENING TIMES:
10–5 daily, (until 6pm
during Easter)
ADM: Adult £9.25,
Child £6.50, Family
£29.50, Conc's £8
GETTING THERE:
Road: M3, M27,
A326, B3054
Train: Brockenhurst
station
FACILITIES:
Restaurant, bar (sea-
sonal), several gift
shops, guided tours
available

THERE ARE TWO quite distinct sides to Beaulieu. A quiet serene side, as represented by the 16th century Beaulieu Palace and its beautiful Lakeside park; and the noisier, more exuberant side of its world famous Motor Museum with its thousands of clanking, clunking, whirring exhibits. Here, at this temple to all things mechanical, you will find exquisitely preserved cars from throughout the history of the motoring age; from late nineteenth century prototypes to ultra modern speed machines. Priceless luxury cars – a 1909 Rolls Royce Silver Ghost or a 1962 E Type Jaguar – sit alongside archetypal people carriers: Volkswagen Beetles, Minis and, of course, the original "people's car", the Ford Model T.

The record breakers of yesteryear are also here, including the 1927 Sunbeam 1000hp, which was the first car to break the 200mph

DISABLED: Access to
all except 2 abbey
buildings, free
wheelchair hire,
toilets
WEBSITE: www.
beaulieu.co.uk

barrier, its once unbelievable feats now long since surpassed.

Elsewhere, you'll find an historic garage and an interactive gallery in which children can unravel the mysteries of the internal combustion engine before sampling the museum's radio controlled cars and hi-tech arcade driving games. A jaunty little monorail makes a regular tour of the palace grounds.

The museum's show piece is its "Wheels" ride which takes you past seven motorised tableaux designed to tell the story of motoring in the twentieth century.

BIRMINGHAM CITY ART GALLERY & MUSEUM

LOCATION:
Chamberlain Square
Birmingham B3 3DH
TEL: 0121 303 2834
OPENING TIMES:
10–5 Mon–Thu &
Sat, 10.30–5 Fri,
12.30–5 Sun
ADM: Free
(contributions wel-
come), charges
apply for Gas Hall
exhibition
GETTING THERE:
Road: M5 J1 & 3; M6
J6
Train: New Street
and Moor Street
stations
FACILITIES: Lots of
car parking space,
Edwardian tea room
and gift shop
DISABLED: Wheelchair
access, Loop system
for hard of hearing,
wheelchair hire,
adapted toilets
WEBSITE: www.
birmingham.gov.uk/
bmag

BIRMINGHAM CITY ART Gallery and Museum is both a collection of art and artifacts from around the world, and a proud promoter of Birmingham's own artistic and industrial heritage. It is home to one of the finest collections of pre-Raphaelite paintings in the world with works by Rossetti Holman Hunt, Millais and Madox-Brown, but also dedicates an entire room to the romantic paintings of local artist Sir Edward Burne Jones. A close friend of William Morris, Burne Jones also turned his hand to stained glass and tapestry design, and is credited with influencing the young Pablo Picasso who, perversely and typically, regarded Burne Jones as a modernist. In the gallery's collection of British art from the 18th to the 20th century, particular prominence is also given to the watercolour landscapes of David Cox, a Birmingham contemporary of Constable. The gallery also holds some of William Morris' original wallpaper designs.

In the museum section, amongst the silverware, jewellery and sculptures is a gallery dedicated to Birmingham's industrial history with various black and oily exhibits from the age of steam. Elsewhere, you can find galleries devoted to natural and social history and a new science gallery which will form part of a Discovery Centre due to open in 2001.

BLACKPOOL PLEASURE BEACH

LOCATION: Ocean Boulevard Blackpool FY4 1EZ
TEL: 0870 444 5566
OPENING TIMES: April–Nov daily 9.30–dusk, Mar, Nov–Dec w/end only
ADM: Free, individual prices for rides, or book of tickets £20.
GETTING THERE: Road: M6 J32; M55 Train: Blackpool North & Blackpool Pleasure Beach stations, change at Preston
FACILITIES: Car parks, shops, various fast food restaurants

HERE, SIZE MATTERS. The BPB is the current Big Daddy of British Tourist attractions, its every vital statistic requiring an "in Britain", "in Europe" or "in the world" suffix. It attracts over 7 million visitors a year which makes it the most popular tourist attraction in Britain, the fourth most popular in Europe and the ninth most popular in the world. In fact, if you discount all attractions which charge an admission fee, the BPB *is* the most popular in the world.

It has the greatest number of rides, 145, of any theme park in Britain and its showpiece ride, the Pepsi Max Big One, is, at a height of 235ft, not only the tallest rollercoaster in the world but also the fastest, capable of travelling at speeds of up to 87mph.

It has the only ride in Britain, the Playstation ride, designed to recreate the effects of being ejected from a fighter plane as well as 10 rollercoasters, a log flume, 45 restaurants and a cabaret lounge.

Its success has given rise to some astounding statistics: each year, BPB visitors consume a

DISABLED: Parking spaces in all car parks, wheelchair access and wheelchair hire.
WEBSITE: www. blackpoolpleasure-beach.co.uk

million ice cream cones, 550,000 burgers and 2.5 million plates of chips and, perhaps as a result, use 20,000 packets of toilet roll.

This love of extremes is perhaps best exemplified by the American Richard Rodriguez who, in August 1998, spent 1013 continuous hours on a BPB rollercoaster; the longest time ever spent riding a rollercoaster, anywhere in the world.

BLACKPOOL TOWER

LOCATION
Central Promenade,
Blackpool,
Lancashire FY1 4BY
TEL: (1253) 622 242
OPENING TIMES:
Easter–early Nov
10–11 daily;
Nov–Easter Sat
10–11, 10–6 Sun
ADM: Adult £7.50,
Child £5.95, Under 4
Free
GETTING THERE:
Road: M6 (J32), M55
Train: Blackpool
North & Blackpool
Pleasure Beach
stations, change at
Preston
FACILITIES:
Shops, bar, various
restaurants
DISABLED: Limited
wheelchair access
WEBISTE: www.
blackpooltourisim.
com/attractions/
blackpool-tower

IN A LITTLE over two centuries, Blackpool has grown from a small hamlet, built next to a "black pool", into the most popular resort in Britain; the heart and symbol of which is its world famous Tower. Built in 1895, and modelled on the Eiffel Tower, it stands a mighty 518ft high. You can take a lift to the to the top from where you can enjoy panoramic views of the coast and Irish Sea.

Following a £13 million face-lift, the Tower now has seven floors stuffed full of attractions including a circus, an aquarium (home to Britain's only giant sea turtles), Jungle Jim's Adventure Playground, a dinosaur theme ride and the beautiful, edwardian Tower Ballroom, as seen on countless editions of *Come Dancing*. Thrill-seekers can try the Walk of Faith, a 5cm thick glass floor, 385ft above the ground.

The tower is perhaps at its most resplendent in September when it becomes the glittering focal point of Blackpool's famous golden mile of illuminations.

BLENHEIM PALACE

LOCATION:
Woodstock, Oxon,
OX20 1PX
TEL: 01993 811 325
OPENING TIMES:
Apr–Oct: 10.30–5.30
daily; park: 9–5 daily
ADM:
Adult £9, Child
£4.50, Family £22.50,
Conc's 7
GETTING THERE:
Road: A44, follow
brown tourist signs
from Oxford 8 miles
south
Train: Oxford station,
then bus 20 from
Oxford Bus station
FACILITIES:
Ample coach and
car parking areas,
gift shops,
restaurant, cafés,
guided tours
DISABLED:
Some wheelchair
access to house and
gardens, adapted
toilets
WEBSITE: www.
blenheimpalace.com

On 13 August 1704, John Churchill, the 1st Duke of Marlborough, lead a 50,000 strong English army to victory in battle against some 60,000 combined French and Bavarian troops at the small town of Blenheim on the River Danube. In recognition of his achievement, a grateful Queen Anne ordered that the Duke be built a new palace in Oxfordshire which he decided to name, appropriately enough, Blenheim.

Designed by Sir John Vanburgh, this huge 14-acre house, with its delicate sandstone colouring and elegant castle-esque pinnacles, is now universally recognised as one of the country's finest examples of Baroque architecture although you can, if you look closely enough, still see evidence of its militaristic origins. The Duke, seemingly unable to resist taking a final swipe at his enemies, ordered that the clock tower be decorated with sculpted images of British lions beating up French cockerels.

These days, Blenheim is most strongly associated in the public imagination with one of the country's other great wartime leaders, Winston Churchill, who was born here in the 19th century. The house contains a display of "Churchiliana", including letters and paintings, in addition to the vast collection of priceless tapestries, antiques, statues and fine furniture that adorn its gilded state rooms.

Blenheim's grounds are, if anything, even more magnificent than the house with neat, sculpted lawns, ponds, fountains, a cascade, water terraces, a symbolic hedge maze and a narrow gauge steam railway leading to a delightful walled pleasure garden.

BRIGHTON PALACE PIER

LOCATION:
Off Madeira Drive,
Brighton BN1
TEL: 01273 609 361
OPENING TIMES:
Summer: 9–2 daily,
Winter: 10–12 daily
ADM: Free, rides are
individually charged
GETTING THERE:
Road: M23 from
London
Train: Brighton
station. (London
Victoria–Brighton
49 mins)
FACILITIES:
3 bars, various fast
food outlets
DISABLED:
Wheelchair access,
toilets
WEBSITE: www.
brightonpier.co.uk

Vaguely reminiscent of an ocean liner on stilts, this beautiful snow-white pier, stretching 1722ft out to sea, was constructed in the 1890's after the original "chain" pier was destroyed in a storm. Much of the filigree iron work remains, as well as some kiosks and a signal cannon from the original pier. In 1931, the pier's first, rather small, Ferris wheel was installed, since when the number and size of the pier's attractions has increased year on year – the only exception was a brief period during World War II, when a section of the pier was dismantled to prevent enemy landings.

Today the Pier manages to combine an old world style and elegance with a more modern knees-up sensibility. There is a roller-coaster, a waltzer, a Ferris wheel, a small go-cart track. a log flume, three bars, a 250 seat fish and chip restaurant and an amusement arcade filled with all the latest video games; plus an inexhaustible supply of such timeless seaside essentials as candy floss, winkles and mussels.

BRIGHTON, THE ROYAL PAVILION

LOCATION:
North Street,
Brighton BN1
TEL: 01273 290 900
OPENING TIMES
Oct–May 10–5,
Jun–Sep 10–6
ADM:
Adult £4.50, Child
£2.75, Conc's £3.25
GETTING THERE:
Road: From London:
M23
Train:
Brighton station
FACILITIES:
Two parking areas
on Church Street;
Queen Adelaide
Tearoom, book and
gift shop
DISABLED:
Wheelchair access,
signed tours by
appointment,
Seinheiser for hard
of hearing, adapted
toilets
WEBSITE:
www.brighton.co.uk

IN 1810, WHEN George III finally succumbed to the madness which had blighted his life and reign for over 30 years, Britain's architecture was dominated by two main schools; neo-Classicism and neo-Gothic. The Prince Regent, later to become George IV, decided to ignore both when he commissioned a new seaside residence to be built in Brighton. Designed by John Nash in the Indian style with a Chinese interior, the result was described by Rev Sidney Smith thus: "it's as though St Paul's had gone down to the sea and pupped".

Neither the Prince Regent nor his chosen architect were great believers in the maxim "less is more" and together they produced a glorious icing sugar concoction of domes, turrets and cast iron palm trees. Recently restored, the sheer opulence of the Pavilion, with its gilded ceilings, vast crystal chandeliers and extravagant frescoes, can at times be a little overwhelming. It's so over-the-top as to be beyond questions of taste and style; just come and rejoice in the excess: pad softly across the music room's hand knotted carpet, gaze at the Banqueting room's chandelier held aloft by a silver dragon, before enjoying a Regency tea in the Queen Adelaide tearoom overlooking the majestic sweep of the newly-restored gardens.

BRITISH AIRWAYS LONDON EYE

LOCATION:
Jubilee Gardens,
The South Bank,
London SE1 75W
TEL: 0870 5000 600
(automated booking
line)
OPENING TIMES:
Apr–Oct: 9–9 daily,
Nov–Mar: 10–6 daily
ADM:
Adult £7.45, Child
£4.95, Conc's £5.95
GETTING THERE:
Underground:
Waterloo,
Westminster
Bus: 12, 53, 76, 77,
109, 211, 507, D1,
P11
FACILITIES:
Gift shop
DISABLED:
Wheelchair access
WEBSITE: www.
ba-londoneye.com

ONE OF THE few Millennium projects that can claim to have been a truly unqualified success, this 450ft rotating observation wheel on the south bank of the River Thames has provided both tourists and London residents alike with whole new way of looking at the capital. Despite a few early problems which saw its maiden turn – originally set for New Year's Eve 1999 – having to be postponed, the wheel has attracted near universal acclaim, its wonderful views and sturdy architecture garnering the sort of reviews that the people behind the Dome could only dream of.

Officially the fourth highest structure in the capital, each of the Eye's 32 enclosed glass-sided capsules (they can hold up to 25 people each) takes around 30 minutes to complete its circumferential journey – the movement is so slow and smooth that there's little chance of travel sickness – allowing you to watch the city gradually unfolding beneath you like a great 3-D tapestry. From the top you can, on a clear day, see for over 25 miles in every direction and, even on an overcast one, you should still be able to make out many of London's most famous landmarks including Canary Wharf, the Telecom Tower and St Paul's Cathedral. And, like the ultimate nosy neighbour, you can even take a peak inside the normally secluded grounds of Buckingham Palace.

THE BRITISH MUSEUM

LOCATION:
Great Russell Street,
London WC1B 3DG
TEL: 020 7636 1555
OPENING TIMES:
10–5 Mon–Sat,
12–6 Sun
ADM: Free, but some
temporary exhibi-
tions make a small
charge

London's great free museum has been delighting and educating the public since 1753. It was then and is now easily the most popular museum in Britain with perhaps the greatest range of archaeological exhibits of any museum in Europe. Its vital statistics alone give some idea of the scope and importance of its collection: the site covers 13½ acres of prime Bloomsbury real estate topped with 7½ acres of roof; there are over 90 permanent and temporary exhibitions that, if you walked around them all, would take you on a trip 2 miles 721 yds long. On your travels

GETTING THERE:
Underground:
Holborn, Russell
Square, Tottenham
Court Road
Bus: 7, 10, 24, 29,
73, 134
FACILITIES: Museum
Tavern, book and
souvenir shop
DISABLED:
Wheelchair access,
adapted toilets
WEBSITE: www.
thebritishmuseum.
ac.uk

you would find perhaps the largest and most comprehensive collection of Egyptian antiquities outside Cairo, a superb Greek and Roman exhibition; a gallery of Japanese decorative art; a priceless collection of medieval illuminated manuscripts as well such singular attractions as the Rosetta Stone, with which scholars finally broke the Egyptian hieroglyphic code; Lindow Man (or Pete Marsh as he is affectionately known), the leathery remains of a 2000 year old Briton; and the ever controversial Elgin Marbles. The famous neo-Classical building which houses this grand collection of global historical memorabilia was built by Sir Sidney Smirke in the mid nineteenth century and recently underwent a £100 million redevelopment resulting in its Great Court being opened to the public for the first time in 150 years (see p.17).

THE BRITISH MUSEUM GREAT COURT PROJECT

IN 2003, THE British Museum will be 250 years old. It decided to celebrate this milestone, and the recent millennium, by commissioning one of the largest and most expensive development projects in its history. The museum's central courtyard, closed to the public for nearly 150 years, re-opened in late 2000 following a thorough architectural transformation. The circular reading room at its centre, which used to house the British Library (now in new multi-million pound premises at St Pancras), now holds a public reference library and exhibition galleries, whilst the surrounding two acres of courtyard have been landscaped and rebuilt to contain a new ethnographic gallery (displaying collections previously housed at the Museum of Mankind) and an education centre, as well as seating areas and cafés. The most stunning development, however, is the new 6,000 sq.m. glass roof, designed by Sir Norman Foster, that arches over the courtyard. Comprised of 3,312 unique triangular panels and weighing some 1,000 tonnes, it makes the courtyard the largest covered public square in Europe.

BUCKINGHAM PALACE

LOCATION:
St James's Park,
London SW1A 1AA
TEL: 020 7839 1377
(general enquiries),
020 7321 2233
(bookings)
OPENING TIMES:
Aug–Sept (exact
dates vary, call in
advance): 9.30–4.30;
entry is by a timed
ticket

For much of the past two centuries Buckingham Palace remained closed to the outside world. This, after all, was the epi-centre of royalty, where the reigning monarchs lived, where knights of the realm were anointed and where OBE and MBE winners went to receive their medals, not some provincial stately home that needed to open its doors in order to make ends meet. Until recently, the closest that most people got to the palace was the front gates, from where they could watch the Changing of the Guard and, on grand state occasions, per-

ADM: Adult £10,
Child £5, Conc's
£7.50
GETTING THERE:
Underground: St
James's Park, Green
Park, Victoria
Bus: 1, 16, 24, 52, 73
FACILITIES:
Souvenir shop
DISABLED:
Special wheelchair
route avoiding stairs,
call in advance
WEBSITE: www.
royal.gov.uk

haps catch a glimpse of the royals themselves parading on the balcony.

Times, however, have changed and the Queen, keen to satiate the public's interest in all things royal, has decided to open the palace's doors for around eight weeks each summer. Only the state rooms can actually be visited – it is unlikely that the private apartments will ever be opened up to public inspection – but these are as opulent and sumptuously decorated as you'd hope. They include the Throne Room – note the pink and yellow coronation thrones of Queen Elizabeth and Prince Philip marked, respectively, with an embroidered EIIR and P – the Marble Hall, the Music Room and, the undoubted highlight, the Picture Gallery which contains works by Van Dyck, Rembrandt, Rubens, Poussin, Vermeer and Canaletto. Remember, if the flag's flying on top of the palace the Queen is in residence.

THE BURRELL COLLECTION

LOCATION: 2060
Pollokshaws Road,
Glasgow G43 1AT
TEL: 0141 649 7151
OPENING TIMES:
10–5 Mon, Wed–Sat,
11–5 Sun
ADM: Free
GETTING THERE:
Road: From South:
M8 J22, M77 J2;

WILLIAM BURRELL, THE great Glasgow shipping magnate, began collecting works of art in 1866 when he was just 15 years old and continued right up until his death in 1958, by which time he had amassed some 8,000 treasures – or roughly two a week.

The collection, housed in a purpose-built building in lovely Pollok Park, is both hugely varied and deeply traditional. Burrell had little time for the avant-garde or experimental side of art; he liked classic lines

from North: M8 J24
Train: Pollokshaws
West station
Bus: 25, 45, 48, 57,
57A from Union
Street
FACILITIES:
Car and coach
parking available
(charges may apply),
gift shop, restaurant,
free guided tours
DISABLED:
Wheelchair access,
adapted toilets

and timeless designs: jewellery from ancient Greece and Egypt, silverware and porcelain from Renaissance Europe and paintings by the great masters. He had a particular penchant for traditional oriental art – Chinese ceramics from the Yuan, Ming and Tang dynasties make up around a quarter of the collection. His most prized items, however, were his medieval tapestries, many of which are over 500 years old.

Burrell's tastes may have been catholic but they were often inspired. There are paintings by Cézanne, Bellini, Monet and Rembrandt as well as a bronze cast of Rodin's "The Thinker". A glimpse into the private life of this most avid of collectors is provided by a reconstruction of the hall and drawing room of the Burrell family home at Hutton Castle, the place where, almost 150 years ago, Burrell's father had attempted to warn his son away from pursuing an "unmanly" interest in art.

CABINET WAR ROOMS

LOCATION: King Charles Street, London SW1A 2AQ
TEL: 020 7930 6961
OPENING TIMES: Apr–Sep: 9.30–6 daily, Oct–Mar: 10–6 daily
ADM: Adult £4.80, Child Free, Conc's £3.60, half price entry for disabled visitors
GETTING THERE: Underground: Westminster, St James's Park
Bus: 3, 109, 159

Down below London's streets in a former government storage basement are 21 cramped, low ceilinged rooms which, for the six years of World War II, were the headquarters of the British war effort. To visit these rooms today is literally to take a step back into the past; they have remained untouched since the final days of the conflict. They are wonderfully evocative; their very smallness (Churchill's office was a converted broom cupboard) giving some sense of the desperate pressure which must have been felt by the men and women who worked here. Each individual detail, so ordinary in itself, becomes, in its context, charged with significance: coloured drawing pins still stuck into faded maps of Europe, papers laid out in the

FACILITIES: Free audio guide, education service and lectures available
DISABLED: Wheelchair access, lift to museum ground floor, adapted toilets
WEBSITE: www. iwm.org.uk

Cabinet Room as if for an imminent briefing, and the desk in Churchill's bedroom from where he made his legendary radio broadcasts. In this small, subterranean patch of London, decisions were made that not only affected the lives of thousands of people but changed the course of history forever.

CADBURY WORLD

LOCATION:
Linden Road,
Bournville,
Birmingham B30 2LD
TEL: 0121 451 4180
OPENING TIMES:
Mid-Feb–Oct: 10–4
daily,
Nov–Mid-Feb: 10–4
Wed, Thu, Sat & Sun
ADM: Adult £6.50,
Child £4.75, Under 4
Free, Family £19.50

SURELY THIS MUST be every child's dream come true, the chance to tour a real chocolate factory *à la* Roald Dahl's Charlie. Your journey begins in a mock rainforest where you can learn how chocolate was first discovered by the invading Spanish Conquistadors being eaten by the Aztecs of South America. They brought the new delicacy back to Europe, where it was soon all the rage in the royal courts prompting an English Quaker family, the Cadburys, to build, in the 19th century, a factory in Birmingham with the intention of providing

GETTING THERE:
Road: M6 J6, M42
J2, off the A38 on
A4040 ring road,
follow the brown &
white tourist signs
Train: Bournville
Station
Bus: 83, 84 & 85
from Birmingham
city centre
FACILITIES:
On-site parking, self-
service restaurant,
chocolate shop
DISABLED:
Wheelchair access
to most of the site
apart form the
packaging plant
WEBSITE: www.
cadbury.co.uk

cheap, mass-produced chocolate for the working classes. As keen advocates of temperance reform, they hoped their confectionery would become an alternative treat to alcohol in the diet of the poor (better fat than drunk seems to have been their logic).

From here, it's on to the more interactive and child-friendly areas of the site to meet giant creme-egg characters, play on chocolate-themed climbing equipment and ride through the chocolate world of Cadabara in a cocoa-bean-shaped car – all the while munching on free chocolate bars.

You can also take a tour of the packaging plant to see chocolate bars being wrapped and watch the careful hand-crafting of luxury chocolates. And, while kids stuff themselves silly, parents can wallow in the nostalgia created by the collection of old sweet wrappers and TVs showing a constant stream of vintage adverts: "A finger of fudge is just enough".

CAERNARFON CASTLE

LOCATION:
Caernarfon,
Gwynedd LL55 2AY
TEL: 01286 677 617

OPENING TIMES:
Apr–Oct: 9.30–6.30
daily, Nov–Mar:
9.30–4 Mon–Sat,
11–4 Sun
ADM: Adult £4,
Family £11, Conc's
£3

GETTING THERE:
Road: A405, A487(T),
B4366
Train: Bangor
station is 9 miles
away
Bus: Buses stop at
the castle itself, call
0891 910 910

FACILITIES: Car and
coach parking,
souvenir and gift
shop

DISABLED: Some
wheelchair access,
call in advance

WEBSITE: www.
caernarfon.com

THE GREAT IRONY of Caernarfon is that, although it is Wales' most famous castle, it was actually built by an Englishman, Edward I, for the purpose of subduing and controlling the Welsh people. Construction began in 1283 following Edward's defeat of Llywelyn ap Gruffydd, the last Welsh Prince of Wales. Conceived as a military stronghold, seat of government and royal palace, Edward wanted his castle to resemble the intimidating walls of Constantinople, the imperial power of Rome and the dream-castle of Welsh myth and legend – no small feat for his chosen architect, James of St George. In military terms, he performed his task ably; the fortress, which bears down over the the walled town of Caernarfon, also founded by Edward, withstood two sieges in the 15th century with a complement of just 28 men-at-arms. Its most striking landmark is the King's Tower, adorned with eagle sculptures and affording an eagle eyed view over the surrounding countryside. The Queen's tower holds the Museum of the Royal Welsh Fusiliers, Wales's oldest regiment. In 1969 the castle was the focus of worldwide attention when the investiture ceremony for Charles, Prince of Wales, was held here and it has subsequently been inscribed on the World Heritage list.

CALLESTOCK CIDER FARM

LOCATION:
Penhallow, Truro,
Cornwall TR4 9LW
TEL: 01872 573 356
OPENING TIMES:
Easter–Jun &
Sep–Oct: 10–6
Mon–Sat, Jul–Aug
9–8 Mon–Fri, 9–6 Sat,
10–6 Sun; Feb–
Easter & Nov–Dec
9–6 Mon–Fri
ADM: Free
GETTING THERE:
Road: It's off the
A3075, follow the
signs from the A30
FACILITIES:
On-site parking,
restaurant, country
wine & cider shop,
jam kitchen & shop,
fruit juice shop,
guided tours
DISABLED:
Wheelchair access
WEBSITE: www.
cornishscrumpy.com

Ask anyone to name the drink they most associate with the West Country and the chances are they will say cider. The image of the Cornish yokel chomping on a corn stork in between gulps of industrial strength scrumpy has become an icon of Englishness, as familiar as cricket on the village green and bicycling bobbies. At Callestock's traditional cider farm you can unravel the mysteries behind this historic drink with a tractor ride through the orchards to see the apple-laden trees and beehives (carefully positioned for maximum chance of pollination) and a visit to the presshouse to watch apples being squelched and bottles being labelled; after which comes the best bit, tasting the cider itself – be warned, it's pretty strong stuff, the farm's motto is not "legless but smiling" for nothing. There's also a cider museum with old apple presses, horse drawn mills and a complete cooper's (barrel maker's) workshop; a farm where you can meet a range of friendly animals including shire horses, Shetland ponies, goats, rabbits and pigs; and a shop where you can sample and buy some of the farm's other produce; the country wines, fruit juices, chutneys, mustard, jams, marmalades, honey and mead that have made this one of the most popular farms in the country.

CANTERBURY CATHEDRAL

LOCATION: Canterbury, Kent CT1 2EH
TEL: 01227 762 862
OPENING TIMES:
Apr–Sep: 8.45–7
Mon–Sat, 12.30–2.30 & 4.30–5.30 Sun;
Oct–Mar: 8.45–5
Mon–Sat, 12.30– 2.30 Sun
ADM: Adult £3,

CANTERBURY, AS BEFITS the administrative, spiritual and theological capital of the English Church, is home to one of the country's most beautiful cathedrals. It looks particularly magical at night when spotlights pick out the detail of the exterior carving.

Most of the building was constructed in the 15th century although parts, including the crypt and some of the stained glass (amongst the very oldest in Britain), date

Child & Conc's £2, Under 5's free, guided tours £3 per person—minimum charge £30
GETTING THERE:
Road: A2, A28
Train: Canterbury West & Canterbury East stations
FACILITIES: audio-visual presentations on "Story of Cathedral": Adult £1, Child & Conc's 70p; permit required to take photos: Adult £1.25, Child & Conc's 70p
DISABLED: Advance notice of wheelchair visits needed
WEBSITE: www.canterbury-cathedral.org

back to the 12th century. Other, later, examples of stained glass feature representations of Thomas à Becket, murdered here in 1170 at the wish, if not the order, of Henry II. After the saint's death, Canterbury became a centre of pilgrimage and catering to the needs of pilgrims became the principal activity of most of the town's inns and taverns, a process described in Chaucer's *Canterbury Tales*. Becket's shrine was destroyed in the 16th century on the orders of Henry VIII following the English church's break with Rome, and his tomb can now be found in Trinity Chapel near the high altar.

During World War II Canterbury was targeted for bombing by Germany as part of its Baedeker Campaign – an attempt to break Britain's will by destroying its most precious religious and cultural landmarks (picked out of a *Baedeker* guide). Miraculously, however, the cathedral and its beautiful stained glass managed to survive the war unscathed.

CHATSWORTH

LOCATION:
Bakewell, Derbyshire
DE45 1PP
TEL: 01246 582 204
OPENING TIMES:
Mid Mar–Oct:
11–5.30 daily
ADM: House &
Garden (including
Scot rooms): Adult
£7.75, Child £3.50,
Family £19, Conc's
£6.50; Garden only:
Adult £3.85, Child
£1.75, Family £9.50,
Conc's £3
GETTING THERE:
Road: M1 J29, M6
J19, off the B6012
Train: Chesterfield
Station, then bus
FACILITIES:
On-site parking (£1
per vehicle), bar,
restaurant, refresh-
ment booth,
tearoom, gift shops
DISABLED:
Wheelchair access
to garden, farmyard
& shop, limited
access to the house

THE "PALACE OF THE PEAKS" is a fitting descrip-
tion for this truly stately home. Every
aspect of the grand 16th-century house and
its Capability Brown-landscaped gardens
exudes a special kind of upper-crust refine-
ment. There are 26 wonderfully ornate rooms
to explore, including nine once used by Mary
Queen of Scots (she stayed here whilst under
the custody of the Earl of Shrewsbury), a large
library and a Dining Room adorned with portraits by Van Dyck, Rembrandt and
Gainsborough. Throughout, the decor is a
heady concoction of marble, gilded leather
and gold leaf. The audio guide, available at
the entrance, will draw your attention
towards some of the more curious items on
display: the table hung with stalactites, the
trompe l'oeil violin, the firescreens used to
stop 19th century ladies' make-up from crack-
ing and the fan made from a Rolls Royce jet
engine (it can produce quite a breeze).

The vast grounds boast over five miles of
walks and trails taking you through kitchen,
rose and cottage gardens, a Serpentine hedge
maze and past a marvellous 200-yd- long
gently tumbling cascade. There are also several attractions for younger visitors including
a fountain made out of a hollowed-out wil-
low tree, a farmyard with goat kids and
lambs to play with and a well-equipped
adventure playground.

CHESSINGTON WORLD OF ADVENTURE

LOCATION:
Chessington,
Surrey KT9 2NE
TEL: 0870 444 777
OPENING TIMES:
Mar–Nov: daily
10–5.15. Last
admission 3pm.
Later closing for
Family Fright Nights
ADM: Adult £19.50,
Child £15.50, Conc's
£10, Disabled/Helper
£9.50

GETTING THERE:
Road: Just off A243;
two miles from A3 &
M25 (J9 from North,
J10 from South)
Train: Chessington
South station,
services from
Waterloo, Clapham
Junction and
Wimbledon

FACILITIES:
Free parking; various
fast food outlets
including McDonalds,
KFC & Pizza Hut

DISABLED:
Safety restrictions
apply on some rides
– a leaflet gives
details. A limited
number of
wheelchairs are
available on request
WEBSITE: www.
chessington.co.uk

CHESSINGTON WORLD OF Adventure began its life as a zoo and there are still a few animals, including lions, gorillas and meerkats, to be found in amongst all the hi-tech gadgetry. These are best viewed from the unusual vantage point provided by the monorail that trundles along above the enclosures. These days, however, natural attractions take second place to mechanical ones. The most intense rides are the 'Samurai' which spins people around on an enormous rotor blade, 'Rameses Revenge', which looks a bit like a great big bread tin and flips its passengers over several times before squirting them in the face with jets of water , and the Vampire, a more traditional rollercoaster-style ride over the park's rooftops. A much gentler excursion is provided by the Mexican-themed Rattlesnake, with its serpent-shaped cars. At the end of each season, on "Family Fright Night" there is an opportunity to sample all these rides in the dark.

Younger children, and those of a less brave disposition, are well catered for at Toytown, the Dragon River Log Flume, Professor Burp's Bubble Works, the Action Man Assault Course and Beanoland, where you can watch costumed characters acting out "comic" scenes.

Reminders of the Park's origins are provided at set times during the day by sealion and penguin displays and at the Creepy Cave where you will find a collection of spiders, insects and other crawling horrors.

CHESTER CATHEDRAL

LOCATION:
Abbey Square, St
Werburgh Street,
Chester CH1 2HU
TEL: 01244 324 756
OPENING TIMES:
7.30–6.30 daily
ADM:
Free (donation of £2
per person recom-
mended)

CHESTER IS NOT a purpose-built cathedral but rather a huge monastic complex which was converted into a cathedral after the dissolution of the monasteries in the mid-16th century. The genesis of the building was slow, organic even. The first Chester church was probably built some time in the 7th century and may have been rebuilt several times over the next few centuries – little evidence from this period survives. What is known is that in 1092 Hugh D'Avranches, the

GETTING THERE:
Road: M56, follow
signs to Chester
Train: Chester
station is a 10-
minute walk away
FACILITIES:
Cathedral shop;
restaurant in 13th-
century Refectory
(sells cathedral's
own-label wine)
DISABLED:
Wheelchair access,
adapted toilets
WEBSITE: www.
chestercathedral.
org.uk

second Norman Earl of Chester (known, not particularly affectionately, as Hugh Lupus, "The Wolf"), began construction of a Benedictine monastic complex.

Building continued for the next 130 years, adapting all the time to changing architectural fashions. The early parts of the complex were classically Romanesque, whilst the later sections are Gothic. Almost as soon as the last building was completed in 1220, the decision was made to rebuild the now stylistically outdated monastic church. This second phase of construction lasted until 1500 and most of the cathedral we see today dates from this period. Despite the huge variety of its architecture, Chester Cathedral hangs together perfectly. It is a wonderfully serene place where visitors can stop and reflect in the quiet ambience of its delightful arcaded cloisters.

CHESTER ZOO

LOCATION:
Upton-by-Chester,
Chester, Cheshire
CH2 12H
TEL: 01244 380 280
OPENING TIMES:
Summer: daily
10–5.30, Winter:
daily 10–3.30
ADM:
Adult £9.50, Child
£7, Family £34,
Conc's £7.50

Britain's largest zoo is home to over 5000 animals spread out over 110 acres of large, natural-looking enclosures. It's a modern establishment, far removed from the traditional menagerie-as-curiosity-shop image. With over 40% of its species classified as endangered, Chester is at pains to point out the importance of its captive breeding programme, the success of which is shown by the hordes of baby animals running around its enclosures. Chester takes its role as an educator seriously and, as with all good teachers, understands that the best way to get people interested in something

GETTING THERE:
Road: M56 J14,
off A41
Train: Chester
Station, then bus
FACILITIES:
On-site parking,
restaurant, self-
service café,
souvenir shop
DISABLED:
Wheelchair access,
audio tours for
visually impaired
WEBSITE: www.
demon.co.uk/
chesterzoo

is by entertaining them. At its regular keeper talks, members of the public are invited to examine some of the zoo's smaller residents and there are feeding displays throughout the day: sea lions at 10.30am and 3.30pm; chimps at 2.15pm; and the ever-popular elephants at 2.30pm and 4pm (a timetable is posted by the entrance). Otherwise, the zoo's showpiece attractions are the penguin pool (you can watch the birds cavorting underwater from a special viewing area); the Twilight World, which contains the largest artificial bat enclosure in the world with over 200 free flying bats; the Monkey Islands (home to mandrills, lion tailed macaques and chimps) and the new "Islands in Danger" exhibition which showcases island-bound endangered species such as Komodo dragons and Birds of Paradise.

Do remember, when planning your itinerary, that the zoo is very large – its 11 miles of pathways will test even the keenest of animal lovers – although you can cut down on your journey time by using the zoo's zippy overhead railway or the waterbus which, in summer, provides close-up views of the lemur and tamarin islands..

COVENT GARDEN

LOCATION:
London WC2
GETTING THERE:
Underground:
Covent Garden,
Leicester Square
Bus: 6, 9, 11, 13, 15,
23, 77A, 91, 176

London Transport
Museum
OPENING TIMES:
10–6 daily, except Fri
when it opens at
11am
ADM: Adult £5.50,
Child & Conc's
£2.95, Under 5 Free,
Family £13.95
FACILITIES:
Café, shop
DISABLED:
Wheelchair access,
adapted toilets
WEBSITE: www.
ltmuseum.co.uk

Theatre Museum
entrance on Russell
Street
OPENING TIMES:
Tues–Sat 11–7
Adm: Adult £4.50,
Child Free, Conc's
£2.50
FACILITIES: Shop
DISABLED:
Wheelchair access
WEBSITE:
theatremuseum.
vam.ac.uk

Apple Market
OPENING TIMES:
9–5 daily (Mon:
antiques; Tue-Fri:
general; Sat-Sun:
crafts)

Jubilee Market
OPENING TIMES:
9.30–6 daily (Mon:
antiques; Tue-Fri:
general; Sat-Sun:
crafts)

L ONDON'S OLDEST SQUARE has been bustling with life for over 300 years now. For much of that time, it was London's cheery bantering heart, the face of honest-to-goodness commerce where the capital's great wholesale fruit 'n' veg' and flower markets thrived. In 1974 the markets relocated and the area underwent redevelopment reopening in 1980. The market buildings were turned into al fresco cafés, boutiques and museums, and the square's pedestrianised confines were reborn as a crafts centre. Today, these gently cobbled streets and cultured shopping arcades are

perhaps London's closest approximation of European street life and café culture.

It contains many attractions starting, at its western end, with St Paul's Church, one of the few major buildings in London to survive the great fire of 1666. Beyond this is the Piazza which provides an informal stage for a constant procession of street performers – jugglers, mime artists, fire eaters, comedians, unicyclists, even the odd musician and busking opera singer. The centrepiece of the square, however, is the 19th-century arcaded market hall, home now to the cheery daily **Apple Market**, which specialises in crafts and clothes, plus a range of cafés, bars, shops and boutiques. The **Jubilee Market**, which deals mainly in tourist souvenirs, can be found in the square's southeast corner, near the **London Transport Museum**, a wonderful collection of vintage buses, trams, tubes and transport memorabilia. The **Theatre Museum** provides a lively trawl through the history of the performing arts, lies just behind.

DUXFORD AIRFIELD MUSEUM

LOCATION:
Duxford, Cambridge,
Cambridgeshire CB2
4QR

TEL: 01223 835 000

OPENING TIMES:
Mid Mar–Mid Oct:
10–6 daily; Mid
Oct–Mid Mar: 10–4
daily

ADM:
Adult £7.40, Child
Free, Conc's £3.70

GETTING THERE:
Road: Just off the
M11 J10, on the
A505
Train: Cambridge
Station, then bus

FACILITIES:
On-site parking,
café, self-service
restaurant (licensed),
gift shops

DISABLED:
Wheelchair access
to most of site
(leaflet available),
adapted toilets

WEBSITE: www.
iwm.org.uk

RUN BY THE Imperial War Museum, Duxford is home to Europe's largest collection of military and civilian aircraft. There are around 180 flying machines in all, ranging from World War I biplanes to the most modern supersonic jet fighters, all housed in seven enormous looming hangars. It's particularly popular with kids who are allowed to climb aboard some of the sleek machines – and no matter what age you are, it's always quite a thrill to sit at the controls of a jet fighter – and put their dog-fighting skills to the test on the hi-tech Battle of Britain simulator. During the real battle, Duxford was one of the country's main fighter aerodromes and you can find out more about the nation's "finest hour" at the restored control tower and operations room. There is also a small section dedicated to land warfare, where you can see reconstructions of battle scenes. and a narrow gauge railway offering trips around the site in summer.

If possible, try to visit during one of the museum's numerous airshows, when you can see the spectacular craft in action – you'll see jets roaring above your head (seemingly only feet away), recreated biplane dog fights and demonstrations of precision formation flying, often as not by the famous Red Arrows.

DYNAMIC EARTH

LOCATION:
Holyrood Road,
Edinburgh EH8 8AS
TEL: 0131 550 7800
OPENING TIMES:
Apr–Oct: 10–6 daily,
Nov–Mar: 10–5
Wed–Sun
ADM: Adult £5.95,
Child & Conc's
£3.50, Family £16.50

ONE OF SCOTLAND'S latest and very best attractions, Dynamic Earth's rather ambitious aim is to provide its visitors with a complete overview of the geological, geographic, biological and sociological history of the earth. Housed in a strange, modern, tent-like building opposite Holyrood House, the exhibition is divided into various zones: the first invites you to travel back inside a "time machine" (actually a lift) to observe the origins of life – wide screen films show the vio-

GETTING THERE:
Road: M8, A1, A70,
A71, A90, follow
signs from city
centre. It's on the
edge of Holyrood
Park opposite
Holyrood House
Train: Waverley
Station
FACILITIES:
On-site parking,
restaurant, shop
DISABLED:
Wheelchair access,
wheelchair helpers
are admitted free
WEBSITE: www.
dynamicearth.co.uk

lent creation of the earth while a hydraulic floor shakes and rolls to simulate a (rather gentle) earthquake, and a mock volcano spews lava and sulphurous gases to the accompaniment of spectacular sound and lighting effects. The next zone demonstrates how different parts of the earth have developed different climates – you can wander from a replica polar region decorated with ice sculptures, to an ersatz rainforest – and how these, in turn, have created an incalculable variety of flora and fauna. It also shows how climate change can often result in mass-extinctions, with models of dinosaurs and sabre-toothed tigers on hand to remind you of past environmental disasters. The final exhibit is a film shown on a vast domed ceiling-screen, detailing the possible catastrophes that could befall the earth if the human race fails to curb its inclination to pollute and destroy the natural environment. Although a little earnest in places, this is a hugely enjoyable exhibition filled with wonderfully imaginative displays that will help you better understand the current state of the planet.

THE EDEN PROJECT

LOCATION:
Bodelva, St Austell,
Cornwall PL24 2SG
TEL: 01726 811 911
OPENING TIMES:
10–6 daily
ADM: Adult £9.50,
Child £4, Under 5
Free, Family £22,
Conc's £5
GETTING THERE:
Road: Just east of St
Austell, signposted
from the A30, A390
and A391
FACILITIES:
On-site parking,
café, shop
DISABLED:
Wheelchair access,
adapted toilets
WEBSITE: www.
edenproject.com

Since Spring 2001, when the Eden Project, the most ambitious botanical scheme ever attempted in this country was completed, Cornwall has had its very own rainforest. In a 60m-deep former china clay pit near St Austell Bay, a vast site, the size of 35 football pitches, has been transformed, at a cost of some £86 million, into the garden to end all gardens. The centrepiece is a series of four giant interconnecting glass and steel conservatories (known as 'biomes'), the largest of which is, at 200m long and 45m high, the biggest conservatory in the world and is filled with plants from the humid tropics — cocoa, bamboo, rubber, teak, mahogany etc. Hi-tech plastic panels control the temperature while sprinklers spray the interior with a fine mist every few minutes in order to mimic the conditions of a real rainforest. Inside it's swelteringly hot and humid and, as you walk through the lush vegetation, it really does feel as you are in the midst of a steaming tropical jungle. This is ecotourism and its most sophisticated. The next largest biome houses warm temperate vegetation — olives, orchids, citrus plants etc — and there's also an outdoor garden supporting a range of native plants and a Visitor Centre containing an exhibition on "the making of Eden" as well as a café and a shop selling organic produce.

EDINBURGH CASTLE

LOCATION: Castle Hill, Old Town, Edinburgh, Midlothian EH1 2NG
TEL: 0131 225 9846
OPENING TIMES: Apr–Sept: 9.30–6 daily; Oct–Mar: 9.30–5 daily
ADM: Adult £6.50, Child £1.80, Conc's £4.80
GETTING THERE: Road: M8, A1, A70, A71, A90 Train: Waverley station is a 5-minute walk away
FACILITIES: Car and coach parking (£2.50 and £5 per vehicle respectively); self-service restaurant, souvenir & gift shops
DISABLED: Reasonable wheelchair access, courtesy vehicle from esplanade, adapted toilets
WEBSITE: www. historic-scotland. gov.uk

Built on a volcanic outcrop 443ft above sea level, Edinburgh Castle has loomed over the city and surrounding countryside for 900 years, defending Scotland and Scottishness from southern encroachments. Architec-turally, the fortress is something of a hotch-potch; the tower and ramparts are of 18th-century origin but there are remains and remnants from every stage of its development. In particular, look out for the beautifully preserved 11th-century chapel of St Margaret.

For centuries the heart of Scotland's defensive system, the castle is home to some of the country's greatest historical and military relics including the Scottish Crown Jewels (much older than their English counterparts), the Stone of Destiny and the medieval siege gun Mons Meg. The castle also houses the Scottish United Services Museum.

As you walk around the castle, you will notice various gruesome landmarks of its murky past, including a spot where over 300 witches were burned and a memorial stone to Sir William Kirkcaldy, whose distinguished career saw him assisting in the murder of Cardinal Beaton and Rizzio, secretary to Mary Queen of Scots (you can visit the Queen's newly restored apartments). Alternatively, should you desire more serene pleasures, you could stand on the battlements and admire the magnificent views over the Firth of Forth.

FLAGSHIP PORTSMOUTH

LOCATION:
Historic Dockyard,
Portsmouth Harbour
Main Office: Porter's
Lodge Building,
1-7 College Road,
HM Naval Base,
Portsmouth PO1 3LJ
TEL:
01705 9286 1533
OPENING TIMES:
Mar–Oct: 10–5.30
daily; Nov–Feb: 10–5
daily

ADM: Ticket to all
attractions: Adult
£14.90, Child £10.90,
Conc's £12.90;
Single ship tickets:
Adult £5.95, Child
£4.45, Conc's £5.20
GETTING THERE:
Road: M27 & M275
then follow brown
Historic Ships signs
through Portsmouth
Train: Portsmouth
Harbour station is a
2-minute walk away
FACILITIES:
Car park, gift shops,
restaurant, adapted
toilets, baby
changing facilities
WEBSITE: www.
flagship.org.uk

Flagship portsmouth is the umbrella organisation which runs Portsmouth's four main naval attractions.

HMS VICTORY

It was aboard this ship that Vice Admiral Nelson commanded the British naval victory at Trafalgar over the combined Franco-Spanish fleet. Fatally wounded in the battle, he was eventually brought home, preserved in a barrel of brandy, to a hero's funeral.

The ship, commissioned in 1759, was the most awesome fighting machine of its day. It carried 100 cannons and was manned by 821 officers and crew including 153 Royal Marines "to provide accurate musket fire in battle". It has been beautifully restored to look exactly as it would have done on that fateful day in 1805. The quarters of Nelson and his friend, Hardy, are particularly rich in period detail.

ROYAL NAVAL MUSEUM

Housed in an 18th-century dockside building, this museum tells the story of the Royal Navy from its beginnings to the Falklands War. As you would expect, there is a good deal of Nelson memorabilia, including his uniform, the furniture from his cabin on HMS Victory, his watch and a miniature of Emma Hamilton. There is also a delightful exhibition tracing the evolution of the sailor's uniform – from frogging and ribands to bell-bottom pants – as well as a new display "Action Stations!" on modern warships.

FLAGSHIP PORTSMOUTH

THE MARY ROSE

IN 1982, WHEN the Mary Rose was raised from the Solent silt in one of the greatest recovery operations in archaeological history, it turned out to be a genuine Tudor time capsule laden with hundreds of unique artifacts. It was built in 1509 on the orders of Henry VIII and was the flagship of the King's fleet in his wars against the French. In 1545 it sank in the Solent during a skirmish and there it lay until rediscovered in 1965. Between 1978 and 1982 much of its contents were recovered; some 19,000 objects made up of a mixture of the ship's military hardware, including heavy guns and longbows (the only examples to survive from Tudor times); and sailors' personal effects: painted pocket sundials, embroidered pouches, rosary beads and lice combs.

HMS WARRIOR

WHEN COMPLETED IN 1861, HMS Warrior was the fastest, most heavily armed, most heavily armoured warship in the world. It was the first to be fitted with an iron hull and the first to carry 110lb guns. Overnight, it made all other warships obsolete and was described by Napoleon III, whose naval threat it had been designed to curb, as "a black snake amongst rabbits". Just 15 years later, however, and without ever having been used in battle, it too was obsolete, surpassed by faster, nastier craft. For much of the 20th century it languished in a state of disrepair and, for a while, even suffered the indignity of becoming a floating pontoon. It was restored to its former splendour in the early 1980s and, in 1987, returned to Portsmouth.

FLAMINGO LAND

LOCATION: Kirby Misperton, Malton, North Yorkshire YO17 0UX

TEL: 01653 668 287

OPENING TIMES: April–Sept: opens 10am, closing times vary according to season, Oct–Mar: weekends and half term only

IN A LITTLE over 20 years, Flamingo Land has been transformed from a small provincial zoo into one of the most popular tourist attractions in Britain. The zoo is still there, larger than ever, with over 180 animal species on display, including Siberian tigers, baboons, zebras, penguins and, of course, flamingoes – although today they share the site with a large fully-equipped theme park.

Flamingo Land is home to some truly terrifying rides known collectively as the

ADM: Adult or Child £12, Under 4's free, Family £42, Conc's £6

GETTING THERE: Road: From South A1, A64, A169; From North A19, A169, A170, Train: Nearest station is Malton Bus: Yorkshire Coastliner from Leeds and Whitby tel 01653 692 556

FACILITIES: Parking, fish and chip shop, Indian takeaway, donuts & ices shop, bar, gift shop

DISABLED: Wheelchair access to park but rides subject to operator's discretion

WEBSITE: www. flamingoland.co.uk

Flamingo Six. These are: the Corkscrew, a 100ft-high loop-the-looper; Wild Mouse, which travels at 28mph along a series of near right-angle bends; the Terrorizer, which is best described as a cross between a roller-coaster and a waltzer; Topgun, a hyper-realistic flight simulator ride; the Bullet, a near vertical rollercoaster; and, top of the heap, the new Para Tower which lifts its passengers 105ft in the air only to release them again for a seriously scary gravity-defying fall to earth. Flamingo Land has developed its own classification system to describe the scariness of its rides. There are five categories: "Challenging", "Teeth Chattering", "Stomach Churning", "Brain Scrambling" and "Bone Crunching". The Bullet, with its unique propulsion system and near vertical descents, is in all five.

Younger children, and adults feeling the need to recover from their exertions, can visit Captain Fortune's Square which offers the gentler pleasures of carousels, a pirate ship boat ride and a haunted castle railway.

FRONTIERLAND

LOCATION:
Marine Road West,
Morecambe Bay,
LA4 4DG
TEL: 01524 410 024
OPENING TIMES:
Mar–Oct, actual
times vary but
usually opens at
10am and closes
between 4pm
and 10pm
ADM: Day Pass High
Season (July–Sept)
£8.95, Low Season
£7.50; Junior Day
Pass High Season
£6.95, Low Season
£5.95; Family Day
Pass High Season
£29.95, Low Season
£25.95; Yippee Night
(selected Fridays
through season)
£2.95; Full Evening
Pass (High Season
only) £5; Junior
Evening Pass £4;
Family Evening Pass
£15
GETTING THERE:
Road: From South:
M6 J35, then A5105;
From North: M6 J34,
then A589
Train: Morecambe
station is 10 minutes
away
FACILITIES:
Free coach parking,
baby changing
facilities, over a
dozen catering
outlets including 2
licensed restaurants
DISABLED:
Wheelchair access
to park and adapted
toilets. Access to
rides is at the
discretion of the ride
operators

BRUSH OFF YOUR spurs, slip on your stetson and utter a loud 'Yee-hah!' in preparation for a visit to this little piece of pioneer-era America transported to northwest England.

There are over 40 rides, each with its own wild west theme: the Texas Tornado, Runaway Mine Train and Stampede are the white-knuckle showpieces, whilst gentler entertainment is provided by the El Paso railroad and crazy-golf course. High steppin' fun

is on offer at the Country Show in the Crazy Horse Saloon and Frontier Fred's Family show – the park is inhabited by a variety of Deputy-Dawgesque rubber-suited characters.

The most strikiing landmark at Frontierlands, however, is strangely out of character with the rest of the park.. The Polo Tower, which has been designed to look like an enormous tube of mints, affords some spectacular views over Morecambe Bay and the surrounding countryside.

GLASGOW MUSEUM & ART GALLERY

LOCATION:
Kelvingrove,
Glasgow G3 8AG
TEL: 0141 287 2699
OPENING TIMES:
10–5 Mon–Sat,
11–5 Sun
ADM: Free
GETTING THERE:
Train:
Nearest station is
Exhibition Centre
Underground:
Nearest station
is Kelvinhall
Bus: 6, 6A, 8, 8C
from George Square;
62, 62B, 62D, 64,
64A from Argyle
Street
FACILITIES:
Car and coach
parking available
(charges may apply),
gift shop, restaurant,
free guided tours
DISABLED:
Wheelchair access,
adapted toilets
WEBSITE: www.
biggarnet.co.uk/tour/
glasgow/museums.
htm

HOUSED IN THE magnificent red brick Kelvingrove mansion, this is one of the world's best city art galleries, with paintings by Botticelli (including his *Annunciation*), Rembrandt, Monet and Van Gogh; sculptures by Rodin and Epstein; and furniture designed by the great Scottish architect, Charles Rennie Mackintosh.

It is neatly complemented by a pleasant little museum where you can find, in the pre-history section, a fabulously detailed reconstruction of the Antonine wall and some beautifully preserved Bronze Age cists. There is also a large natural history section as well as hordes of silver, silver plate, porcelain, and a number of suits of armour.

The Kelvingrove mansion itself was built in 1901 with proceeds received from an exhibition held in Kelvingrove Park. Today, visitors to the museum can wander through the gorgeous 85 acres parkland down to the River Kelvin where, in summer, concerts are held in the amphitheatre.

GLOUCESTER DOCKS

LOCATION: Gloucester, Gloucestershire GL1

GETTING THERE:
Road: M5 J11, J12 or J12a, then A38, A40. Follow brown and white tourist signs
Train: Gloucester Station, 10-minute walk

FACILITIES:
On-site parking, cafés, restaurants

National Waterways Museum, Llanthony Warehouse
TEL: 01452 318 054
OPENING TIMES: 10–5 daily
ADM: Adult £4.75, Child & Conc's £3.75, Family £11
FACILITIES: Café, shop
DISABLED: Wheelchair access
WEBSITE: www.nwm.org.uk

Robert Opie Collection
TEL: 01482 302 309
OPENING TIMES: Mar–Sep: 10–6 daily; Oct–Feb: Tues–Sun 10–5
ADM: Adult £3.50, Child £1.25, Family £8.50, Conc's £2.30
FACILITIES: Shop
DISABLED: Wheelchair access

Soldiers of Gloucestershire Museum
TEL: 01452 522 682
OPENING TIMES: 10–5 Tue–Sun & Bank Hol Mon
ADM: Adult £3.50, Child £1.90, Conc's £2.50
FACILITIES: Shop
DISABLED: Wheelchair access

IN THE MID-18TH century Gloucester's docks, the most inland in the country, hummed with activity inspired by a thriving sea trade. A mere 100 years later, however, under fierce competition from nearby Bristol, this trade had all but dried up and the docks (and consequently the city) fell into decline. Happily, today, they have been reborn as a sort of cultural-cum-shopping centre; the grand Victorian warehouses now home to a shop-

ping mall, a well-respected antiques centre, various bars, cafés and restaurants as well as several excellent museums. There's the *National Waterways Museum* which has three floors full of interactive exhibits, audio-visual displays and waxwork dioramas designed to bring the history of the country's canals and docks to life. You can explore the interior of a narrowboat to see how canal families used to live, try on a diver's helmet and watch the resident blacksmith at work in his forge. You can even take a tour of the Gloucester and Sharpness Canal aboard the museum's own sightseeing boat, the Queen Boadicea II. At the snappily titled *Robert Opie Collection – Museum of Advertising and Packaging* you can take a stroll down memory lane among its extensive collections of historic packets, tins, bottles, comics and advertisements all arranged in re-created shop interiors. The collection contains items dating back to 1870, allowing you to see how the design of a particular product such as Bovril or Colman's Mustard has changed over the course of a century – as well as an antique TV showing a continuous stream of vintage commercials. The nearby *Soldiers of Gloucestershire Museum* tells the story of the Glosters and the Royal Gloucestershire Hussars through a mixture of films, photographs and life-size displays including a recreated World War I trench.

HAMPTON COURT GARDENS

ADM: **Free when visiting the gardens only**

HAMPTON COURT'S SUPERB landscaped gardens were started by Henry VIII back in the early 16th century. Their current form and lay-out, however, is mostly the result of work undertaken during the reign of William III and modifications made by the great royal gardener Lancelot "Capability" Brown in the 18th century. It contains many wonders: a 1,000-year-old oak tree, the oldest and longest vine in the world, planted in 1768 (in the early part of this century the grapes were harvested in baskets made by soldiers blinded in World War I), 100,000 rose bushes, 250,000 flowering bulbs and, of course, the most famous maze in the world. It was planted in 1690 for William III and lures in around 300,000 people a year (and lets roughly the same number out again, give or take a few). It takes about 20 minutes to reach the centre of the maze and at least double that to negotiate your way back through the $1/3$ acre of yew-lined paths. No wonder, then, that these are the most popular gardens in Britain, attracting around 1.3 million people a year.

HAMPTON COURT PALACE

LOCATION:
Surrey, KT8 9AU
TEL: 020 8781 9500
OPENING TIMES:
Oct–Mar: 10.15– 4.30
Mon, 9.30– 4.30
Tue–Sun; Mar–Oct
10.15–6 Mon,
9.30–6 Tue–Sun
ADM: Adult £10.50,
Child £7, Under 5's
free, Family ticket
£31.40, Conc's £8

HAMPTON COURT, ONE of the most famous and best-loved of all royal palaces, hasn't actually had a royal in residence for over 250 years. Despite its undoubted magnificence, the typical regal attitude towards it has been at best ambiguous and at times downright hostile. The construction of the palace began when Henry VIII seized the Hampton estate from his chief advisor, Cardinal Wolsey, having earlier refused it when offered to him as a gift.

Over the next ten years, Henry spent more than £62,000 (that's around £18 million in

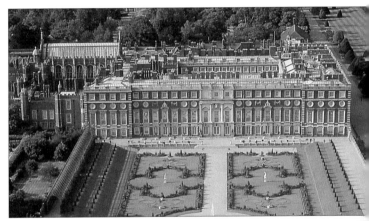

GETTING THERE:
Road: From London:
A3, A309 to Esher/
Staines, then follow
signs. From M25:
Exit 12 for M3
towards London,
Exit J1, A308 to
Kingston, then
follow signs
Train: Hampton
Court station
FACILITIES:
Car park (£3 charge),
shops, restaurant,
café, guided tours
available
DISABLED:
Wheelchair access,
disabled parking,
adapted toilets
WEBSITE: www.
hrp.org.uk

today's money) on rebuilding work. By the time he had finished, he had created the most modern, sophisticated palace in England with a real tennis court, a bowling alley, a vast 36,000 sq ft kitchen (staffed by 200 people), pleasure gardens and, perhaps its greatest feature, a multiple lavatory which could seat 28 people at a time and was known as "The Great House of Easement". The next monarch to take an interest in the palace was William III, 150 years later. He instigated further rebuilding work, this time costing a mere £131,000 (today £9.5 million), the most important element of which was the planting of new gardens and a maze. Of subsequent monarchs, only George II made use of the palace and in 1838 it was opened to the public.

Today, visitors can wander around the vast 50-room Tudor kitchen, the wonderfully elaborate King's staircase, the fountain court (the centrepiece of William III's palace reconstruction) and a Renaissance picture gallery containing works by Brueghel and Mantegna.

IMPERIAL WAR MUSEUM

LOCATION:
Lambeth Road,
London SE1 6HZ
TEL: Enquiries 020
7416 5320, Infoline
0891 600 140
OPENING TIMES:
10–6 daily
ADM: Adult £5,
Child £2.50,
Conc's £4, Family
ticket £13; free entry
after 4.30pm

Tʜɪs ᴍᴜsᴇᴜᴍ, ᴅᴇᴅɪᴄᴀᴛᴇᴅ to tracing the history of civilisation's great madness, is housed, appropriately enough, in what was formerly the Bedlam lunatic asylum.

The museum makes no attempt to treat conflict as some sort of great Boys Own adventure. Instead, the displays tend to focus on the human experience of war as illustrated by two excellent exhibitions: the Trench Experience, a vivid recreation of the life of an ordinary footsoldier holed up beneath the Flanders mud; and the Blitz Experience which, with the aid of some special sound

GETTING THERE:
Underground:
Lambeth North,
Elephant & Castle
Train: Waterloo,
Elephant & Castle
Bus: 1, 3, 12, 45,
53, 63, 68, 159, 168,
171, 172, 176, 188,
344 & C10
FACILITIES:
Café, gift/bookshop
DISABLED:
Wheelchair access,
the cinema has
infra-red audio
enhancement
WEBSITE: www.
iwm.org.uk

and visual effects, goes some way towards illustrating the terrors and privations of an aerial siege.

There is, of course, plenty of hardware on display in the large central hall including tanks, planes (many of which you can climb inside) and even a 30ft Polaris missile which, shorn of their movement and function, now seem rather innocuous and tasteful, as well as a number of touch-screen computers on which you can watch archive footage of past conflicts.

Perhaps the most affecting part of the museum, however, is the recently opened Holocaust Exhibition in the new 6-storey extension. Story boards, film clips, first-hand accounts as well as artifacts from the concentration camps together paint a powerful and moving portrait of one of the great horrors of the 20th century

JORVIK VIKING CENTRE

LOCATION:
Coppergate, York,
North Yorkshire
YO1 1NT
TEL: 01904 643 211
OPENING TIMES:
Daily; 1 Jan–12 Feb:
9–3.30; 13 Feb–
21 Feb: 9–5.30;
22 Feb–26 Mar:
9–3.30; 27 Mar–
31 Oct: 9–5.30;
1 Nov–31 Dec:
10–4.30
ADM: Adult £5.35,
Child £3.99, Under
5's free, Family £17,
Conc's £4.59
GETTING THERE:
Road: A1036, A1079
Train: York station
FACILITIES:

THE JORVIK VIKING Centre is a unique archaeological experience where visitors have the opportunity to ride through a time tunnel to see the sights, hear the sounds and even smell the smells of a 10th-century Viking village. Between 1976 and 1981 the York Archaeological Trust unearthed, in the centre of York, the greatest collection of Viking remains ever found in Britain – a find so large that it merited the construction of a museum all to itself. This was to be no ordinary museum, however, with rows of glass cases stuffed full of dusty fragments and indeterminate relics. Instead, it was to hold a full-scale recreation of a Viking settlement, painstakingly designed to look exactly as it would have done 1,000 years ago.with thatched huts, workshops, alleys and wharfs inhabited by accurately rendered models of the Vikings themselves: tradesmen, craftsmen, fishermen and their families arranged in a series of everyday tableaux. To complete

Gift shop and café
DISABLED:
Wheelchair access
WEBSITE: www.
jorvik-viking-centre.
co.uk

the picture, authentic sound and smell effects were added. The result is an intense, hyper-real Viking universe. "Time cars" carry the visitors through the recreated village along a magnetic track.

There is also a reproduction of the laboratory where the scientific research for the project was carried out and a more traditional gallery where you can see some of the dig's better preserved items, including examples of Viking jewellery.

KENILWORTH CASTLE

LOCATION:
Castle Green,
Kenilworth,
Warwickshire CV8
1NE

TEL: 01926 852078
Opening Times:
April–Oct Mon–Sun
10–6, Nov–Mar
Mon–Sun 10–4
Adm: Adult £3.50,
Child £1.80, Conc's
£2.60

GETTING THERE:
Road: It's on the
western edge of
Kenilworth town, off
the A46. Follow the
signs.

TRAIN: The nearest
train station is
Coventry, from
where you'll have to
catch a bus, call
01926 414140

FACILITIES: On-site
parking, Tudor barn
café, gift shop

DISABLED: Some
wheelchair access

WEBSITE: www.
englishheritage.org.
uk

There's something distinctly organic-looking about the great sandstone bulk of Kenilworth Castle. Rising out of the Warwickshire countryside like a set of gnarly red dentures, it both towers above, and yet seems an intrinsic part of, the surrounding landscape. Begun in the 12th century, the castle reached the pinnacle of its status in the late 1500s when it was the home of Robert Dudley, the Earl of Leicester (and Elizabeth I's favourite courtier), who spent vast sums on the structure turning it into one of the most splendid palaces in Europe. The castle's fortunes declined markedly in the next century, however. Badly damaged during the Civil War, it was subsequently abandoned and allowed to fall into disrepair — its buildings crumbled, its great lake dried up and its gardens became wild and overgrown.

Despite centuries of neglect, the castle is still an impressive sight — indeed, it's the country's largest ruined castle — and its grand craggy walls provide wonderful views of the surrounding countryside. Parts of the Norman Tower, Strong Tower and Great Hall survive as does much of the encircling curtain wall and you can walk through a reconstruction of the original Tudor gardens. The former stables now hold a shop and cafeteria.

Audio guides are available and, in summer, the castle stages a variety of activities and events including demonstrations of medieval combat, plays and performances of Tudor music.

KENSINGTON PALACE

LOCATION:
Kensington Gardens,
London W8 4PX
TEL: 020 7376 2858
OPENING TIMES:
Mid Mar–mid Oct:
10–6 daily, mid
Oct–mid Mar: 10–5
ADM: Adult £9.50,
Child £7.10, Family
£29.10, Conc's £6.70
GETTING THERE:
Underground: High
Street Kensington,
Bayswater,
Queensway
Bus: 9, 10, 12, 52,
73, 94
FACILITIES:
Orangerie tearoom,
souvenir shop
DISABLED: Limited
wheelchair access,
adapted toilets
WEBSITE: www.
hrp.org.uk

IN THE WEEKS following Princess Diana's death in 1997, the gardens outside her home at Kensington Palace became the focus for a nation's grief. Adorned with thousands and thousands of bunches of flowers, they were for a short time the most photographed site in the world. Although people continue to leave flowers at its gates, the palace has resisted the temptation to become a Diana memorial like her family home at Althorp. Instead, it provides a fascinating glimpse into three centuries of royal fashion. At its "Dressing for Royalty" exhibition you can see both the extravagant costumes of the royals themselves – most notably the magnificent coronation robes of George V and Queen Mary as well as 16 dresses owned by the present Queen – and those worn by young society ladies presented at court during the debutante season; fabulous, glittering creations adorned with pearls and gems that were the result of days of finger-numbing work by seamstresses.

The palace itself was built in the late 17th century for William III and Mary and, in the 19th century, was the childhood home of the future Queen Victoria. Today, you can tour the upper floor state apartments in the company of an audio guide to see the room where the young princess was told of her accession to the throne, the King's Staircase built by Sir Christopher Wren, and the lavishly decorated Cupola Room. You can also visit the lovely sunken garden.

KEW GARDENS

LOCATION:
Kew, Richmond,
Surrey TW9 3AB
TEL: 020 8332 5622
Infoline
020 8940 1171
OPENING TIMES:
9.30–dusk
ADM: Adult £5,
Child £2.50, Under
5's free, Family ticket
£13, Conc's £3.50,
blind, partially sight-
ed and wheelchair
users free

I T'S THE MIDDLE of winter, there's a chill in the air, snow on the ground and dark grey clouds overhead, but without the time or money to take that trip to the Caribbean there's precious little to do except wrap up warm and pray for spring. Alternatively, you could pay a visit to the one part of London where tropical weather is guaranteed 365 days a year. And after ten minutes spent in the sweltering heat of the Palm House, a huge Victorian conservatory where the conditions are designed to mimic those of a tropical rainforest, you'll never complain about a British winter again.

The Royal Botanic Gardens, spread over a 300-acre site on the south bank of the

GETTING THERE:
Train: Kew Bridge,
Kew Gardens
Underground:
Kew Gardens
Bus: 65, 391, 267,
R68 (Sun only)
FACILITIES:
Baby-changing
facilities; 2 gift
shops, 2 self-
service restaurants,
coffee bar, bakery,
snack shop
DISABLED:
Wheelchair access,
adapted toilets
WEBSITE: www.
kew.org

Thames, have grown over the course of their 200-year history into the largest and most comprehensive collection of living plants in the world, containing representatives of more than 1 in 8 of all flowering plants. All year round, these beautifully manicured grounds provide a dazzling display of blooms, from crocuses, camellias and bluebells in spring to strawberry trees and witch hazel in winter. There are three enormous conservatories: the above-mentioned Palm House (the most important surviving 19th-century glass and iron structure in the world), the late-Victorian Temperate House, and the Princess of Wales Conservatory, built in the 1980s and home to both the giant Amazonian water lily and *Titan Arum*, the largest, and quite possibly the smelliest, flower in the world. There is also a ten-storey, 165ft-high 18th-century pagoda.

KNOWSLEY SAFARI PARK

LOCATION:
Prescot, Merseyside,
L34 4AN
TEL: 0151 430 9009
OPENING TIMES:
Mar–Oct: 10–4 daily
ADM: Adult 7, Child
& Conc's £5, Under 3
Free
GETTING THERE:
Road: M62 exit 6,
M57 exit 2
Train: The nearest
station is Lime
Street in Liverpool
FACILITIES:

OPENED IN 1971 by the 18th Earl of Derby, this was the first safari park in Britain to be built near a major city – just eight miles from the centre of Liverpool. A series of moats and electric fences prevents the animals from putting in any unexpected appearances in the high street.

In the mid 19th-century the 13th Earl of Derby kept one of the largest private collections of animals in the world on this site. Members of the public could visit, in groups of no more than six, only with the written permission of the Earl. Today the park's authorities are much more accommodating. The full 'Safari' experience takes you on a five-mile ride through the park's enclosures,

Coach and car
parking available on
site, baby changing
rooms, fairground,
restaurant, souvenir
and gift shop
DISABLED:
Wheelchar access
(apart from railway),
adapted toilets
WEBSITE: www.
knowsley.com

home to the largest herd of elephants in Europe, wildebeest, buffalo, zebra and rhinos (known collectively, rather appropriately, as a 'crash', the park is one of only a handful in the world to have successfully reintroduced rhinos bred in captivity into the wild) as well as ostriches, camels and a troop of baboons. You are allowed to travel past but not through the lion and tiger enclosures.

Elsewhere in the park is a children's fun-park, a small steam railway and a show area for daily sea lion performances.

LEEDS CASTLE

LOCATION:
Maidstone, Kent
ME17 1PL
TEL: 01622 765 400
OPENING TIMES:
Castle Mar–Oct:
11–5.30, Nov–Feb:
10.15–3.30; Park &
Gardens Mar–Oct:
10–5, Nov–Feb: 10–3
ADM: Adult £9.50,
Child £6, Family £26,
Conc's £7.50; Park &
Gardens only: Adult
£7.50, Child £4.50,
Faily £21, Conc's £6

HENRY VIII'S FAVOURITE royal residence, Leeds is one of Britain's great castles. Set on two islands in the middle of a lake in 500 acres of beautifully sculpted Kent countryside, the castle provides an architectural summary of the last 1,000 years. The cellar dates from the 11th century, the Gatehouse from the 12th (within is a collection of dog collars, some of which are over 400 years old), the Maiden's Tower is Tudor whilst the main residential quarters were built in the last century.

There was a manor on this site back in the 9th century but it wasn't until 1119, following the Norman invasion, that the construction of a stone castle began. Both Edward I and Edward III left their mark, but it took the

GETTING THERE:
Road: M20 J8
Train: Nearest
station is Bearsted,
Eurostar stops
at Ashford
International,
20 minutes away
FACILITIES:
Gift, clothing
and plant shops,
restaurant, picnic
area, golf course
DISABLED: Some
wheelchair access,
disabled car
parking spaces
WEBSITE: www.
leeds-castle.co.uk

largesse of Henry VIII, who spent a fortune on enlarging the castle and beautifying the grounds, to turn the castle into one of the most splendid fortresses in Europe. Today, visitors can get some sense of the castle's former opulent glory in Henry's 72ft Banqueting Hall with its ebony wood floors and carved oak ceiling and in the Queen's bedroom, furnished to look as it would have done when occupied by Catherine de Valois, Henry V's wife.

Within the enchanting grounds are a maze, a grotto, a duckery, a vineyard, greenhouses and even a golf course. Throughout the year, the grounds play host to various special events including wine festivals, open air concerts and, of course, the famous Leeds Balloon Festival when the sky around the castle becomes filled with dozens of weird and wonderfully shaped hot air balloons.

LEGOLAND

LOCATION: Windsor, Berkshire SL4 4AY
TEL: 08705 047 0404
OPENING TIMES: 10–6 daily, park closes 8pm between mid Jul–Aug
ADM: Adult £18, Child £15
GETTING THERE: Road: 2 miles from Windsor on the Windsor to Ascot Road, close to M4, M3, M25
Train: Riverside, Windsor Central
FACILITIES: 7 restaurants/cafés and 11 catering stalls
DISABLED: Wheelchair access, wheelchair hire available, adapted toilets
WEBSITE: www. lego.co.uk

FAST BECOMING ONE of the country's top family attractions, Legoland is perhaps best described as a cross between a theme park and an activity centre. It has some great thrill rides including a dragon-themed rollercoaster which jets its way through a mock medieval castle and a log flume 'Pirate Falls'. The most popular attractions, however, those designed to get the under 12s jumping with joy, are the interactive zones such as Lego Traffic, where children have the chance to drive electrically powered Lego cars through a model town, negotiating traffic lights, pedestrian crossings and roundabouts on the way – the most skillful drivers are awarded their own special Legoland Driving License – and the Imagination Centre where kids are encouraged to indulge in creative play, which translates as erecting model buildings and then destroying them on a special Earthquake Table. Older children can create robotic models using the rather eerie concept of "intelligent" lego bricks at the Mindstorm Centre, whilst their younger siblings run riot in the Duplo Gardens.

Perhaps the most intriguing section, for children and adults alike, is Miniland with its beautifully rendered model cities – London, Amsterdam, Brussels *et al*. It took 100 model makers 3 years to complete and is made up of no less than 20,000,000 Lego blocks.

LONDON AQUARIUM

LOCATION:
County Hall,
Riverside Building,
Westminster Bridge
Rd, London SE1 7PB
TEL: 020 7967 8000
OPENING TIMES:
10–6 daily
ADM: Adult £8.50,
Child £5, Family £24,
Conc's £6.50
GETTING THERE:
Underground:
Waterloo,
Westminster
Bus: 12, 53, 76, 77,
109, 211, 507, D1,
P11
FACILITIES: Shop
DISABLED:
Wheelchair access,
adapted toilets
WEBSITE: www.
londonaquarium.co.uk

UNTIL 1986, ONLY political animals were found in County Hall. Today, however, the former offices of the Greater London Council are home to thousands of different creatures from all over the world: sharks, eels, rays and jellyfish, all of which can be seen swimming their way around the huge, million-gallon tanks of the London Aquarium. Arranged according to habitat and region, the aquarium has displays on freshwater rivers, coral reefs, mangrove swamps and rainforests, as well as tanks holding representatives from the Indian, Pacific and Atlantic oceans. You'll see sharks turning lazy circles around the Pacific tank as well as many creatures perhaps best categorised under the heading, "beautiful but deadly": tiny green poison arrow frogs, intricately camouflaged stone fish, puffy faced porcupine fish and, most deadly (and beautiful) of all, lion fish which have so many fins and spines that they look like nothing so much as rather spiky, crumpled silk scarves.

More interactive pleasures can be found at the touch pool where visitors are invited to stroke the alien-looking (but still rather cute) rays, who seem to get a dog-like satisfaction from the experience. Dotted in among the tanks, are a number of computer terminals where you can find out more about the Aquarium's inhabitants. There are touch screen quizzes and short-play videos in which cartoon sea creatures explain themselves and their environment to visitors: "Hi, I'm a conch, I live at the bottom of the sea...".

LONDON DUNGEON

LOCATION:
28–34 Tooley Street,
London SE1 2SZ
TEL: 020 7403 7221
OPENING TIMES:
Apr–Sep: 10–5.30
daily, Oct–Mar:
10.30–5 daily
ADM: Adult £9.50,
Child & Conc's £8.50
GETTING THERE:
Underground:
London Bridge
Bus: 10, 44, 48, 70,
133
FACILITIES:
Café, souvenir shop
DISABLED:
Wheelchair access
WEBSITE: www.
dungeons.com

THE DARK, GLOOMY railway arches of London Bridge Station provide an appropriately sinister setting for this celebration of the macabre. Inside the dark, candlelit "dungeon", you are invited to explore a series of gruesome waxwork tableaux depicting some of the more grisly episodes from British History: a human sacrifice by druids at Stonehenge, Boadicea stabbing a Roman soldier to death, Anne Boleyn being beheaded (in the middle of her farewell speech, according to legend her lips continued to say the words for several seconds after her head had been separated from her body) as well as the blotchy, bloated victims of the great plague and the manacled maniacs of Newgate Prison. The highlight, however, is a graphic recreation of the life and times of everyone's favourite serial killer, Jack the Ripper. You can walk the streets where his infamous crimes took place and hear the muffled cries of his victims – it ends with a spectacular computer generated fireball. There's also an array of medieval torture instruments to "admire", including a mantrap, an iron maiden and a Halifax Gibbet (a sort of prototype guillotine), as well as a new water ride, Judgment Day, which sails you through a replica of Traitors' Gate in the nearby Tower of London to await execution. Definitely not for the squeamish – it's probably not a good idea to take very young children or anyone (young or old) susceptible to nightmares.

LONDON PLANETARIUM

LOCATION:
Marylebone Road,
London NW1 5LR
TEL: 020 7935 6861
OPENING TIMES:
Shows run every 40
mins from 12.20–5;
weekends and
school holidays
from 10.20am
ADM: Adult £6, Child
£4, Conc's £4.60;
combined
Planetarium/
Madame Tussaud's
ticket: Adult £12.25,
Child £8,
Conc's £9.30
GETTING THERE:
Underground:
Baker Street
Bus: 18, 27,
30, 74, 159
FACILITIES: Gift shop
DISABLED:
Wheelchair access,
induction loop for
the hard of hearing
WEBSITE: www.
madame-
tussauds.com

The Planetarium has been using state-of-the-art technology to explain the mysteries of the cosmos for over 40 years now. It's split into two parts, a museum and an auditorium. In the former, which is known as the 'Planet Zone', you can see waxworks of Neil Armstrong and Buzz Aldrin, the first men on the moon, watch live satellite weather transmissions from space telescopes, and step on to a special set of scales which tells you what your weight would be on the moon (where, happily, everyone is much lighter). There are also numerous video and audio displays where you can hear such astral luminaries as Stephen Hawking and Patrick Moore giving their opinions on the great beyond. Interesting thought this section is, it's really just an hors d'oeuvre to the celestial main course — the £1 million Planetary Quest 3D extravaganza in the world-famous dome, that takes you on a whizz-bang tour of the galaxy past exploding supernovas, whirling starfields and crashing asteroid belts. The animation is based on data received from the Hubble Space Telescope and Voyager Space Probe. Throughout the year, the planetarium puts on regular live programmes with a range of guest speakers.

LONDON ZOO

LOCATION: Regent's Park, London NW1 4RY
TEL: 020 7722 3333
OPENING TIMES: Summer: 10–5.30 (last admission 4.30pm); winter: 10–4 (last admission 3pm)
ADM: Adult £9, Child £7, Under 4's free, Family ticket £28, Conc's £8
GETTING THERE: Train: Camden Road Underground: Regent's Park, Camden Town, Mornington Crescent, Baker Street Bus: 274, C2. Waterbus also runs along Regent's Canal (hourly 10–5 every day).
FACILITIES: Parking, baby-changing facilities, café, various fast food outlets, gift and souvenir shop
DISABLED: Some wheelchair access, adapted toilets
WEBSITE: ww . webolife.co.uk

Did you know that the elephant has 60,000 muscles in its trunk? Or that the sparrow has twice as many bones in its neck (14) as a giraffe? Or that the swan has more feathers (25,000) than any other species of bird? If you did, it's probably because you've recently paid a visit to London Zoo, still the best place for people to come and learn about the creatures that share their planet.

The modern London Zoo is first and foremost a scientific institute and conservator of endangered species. Nonetheless, it still makes the majority of its revenue through turnstile

receipts, which means it must continue to display its animals in a way that is both attractive to the public and consistent with its remit. Thankfully, this is exactly what it does. Everyday the zoo organises talks and "Meet the Animals" sessions. Turn up at feeding time and you can watch pelicans and penguins gobbling their way through buckets of fish or a snake slowly swallowing a rat – whole. If you're very lucky, you might even see an elephant taking a bath.

Spectacular animal shows are held in two special demonstration areas – you can see monkeys, lemurs and parrots leaping, climbing and flying – while at the zoo's latest attraction, the "Web of Life", you can see how various animals, plants and organisms combine to form ecosystems. There are examples of different habitats from around the world – a mangrove swamp, a seashore, a coral reef, an underground burrow, a dung heap – with bubble windows and magnified tanks allowing you to immerse yourself in the animals' environments.

MADAME TUSSAUD'S

LOCATION:
Marylebone Road,
London NW1 5LR
TEL: 020 7935 6861
OPENING TIMES:
10–5.30 Mon–Fri,
9.30–5.30 Sat–Sun;
earlier opening
during summer
ADM:
Adult £10, Child
£6.50, Conc's £4.60;
Combined ticket
with Planetarium:
Adult £12.25, Child
£8, Conc's £9.30
GETTING THERE:
Underground:
Baker Street
Bus: 18, 27,
30, 74, 159
FACILITIES:
Gift shop, café,
Thomas Cook
Bureau de Change
DISABLED:
Wheelchair access
WEBSITE: www.
madame-
tussauds.com

Set amongst the stuccoed terraces that surround Regent's Park, this is the grand temple of waxwork kitsch. The 2.5 million visitors who pass through its doors each year get to explore four floors stuffed full of ersatz celebrities, featuring everyone from Dr Crippen to Princess Anne.

The museum itself is divided into five themed areas including the Garden Party, the Grand Hall, the Spirit of London – a sort of tableaux funfair in which you are carried in a mock-up London taxi through representations of London history from Elizabethan times to the present day –

and, of course, the Chamber of Horrors with its collection of gruesomely rendered murderous favourites.

Madame Tussaud established her reputation in the late 17th century making wax portraits of the French aristocracy. Thrown in jail during the Revolution (the 1780s were not a good time to start cosying up to the nobility), she was released on the condition that she sculpted the death masks of the Revolution's more celebrated victims.

In 1802 she moved to England where she spent the next 33 years touring her models around the country until, in 1835, a permanent site was found for them in Baker Street – the museum moved to its present location in 1885. She died in 1850 aged 89. Her last work, a rather eerie self-portrait, is still on display in the Grand Hall.

MUSEUM OF SCIENCE & INDUSTRY MANCHESTER

LOCATION: Liverpool Road, Castlefield, Manchester, Greater Manchester M3 4FP
TEL: 0161 832 2244
OPENING TIMES: 10–5 daily
ADM: Adult £6.50, Child Free, Conc's £3.50
GETTING THERE: Train: Deansgate Station, G-Mex Metrolink, both a 5 minute walk away Bus: No.33
FACILITIES: Some on-site parking, restaurant, café, souvenir shop
DISABLED: Wheelchair access, adapted toilets
WEBSITE: www.msim.org.uk

Once upon a time, Manchester was the brightest furnace burning in Britain's "workshop of the world". The spiritual home of the factory, it now provides the perfect setting for a museum dedicated to tracing the history of industrial invention. From spinning jennies to supersonic jets, this is nothing less than a complete overview of the inexorable progress of physical science. Its centrepiece is an 1830 railway station – the oldest such building in the world – around which is grouped a collection of 19th-century brick warehouses filled with the great metal behemoths of the industrial age: steam engines, railway locomotives (stream train trips are given along a short stretch of line on Sundays during the summer), vintage cars and, appropriately enough for a city founded largely on the back of the textile industry, looms. You'll find displays on electricity, the history of photography and TV as well as a four-storey transport gallery with an Air & Space section that runs the gamut from biplanes to space stations. Although largely concerned with the technologies of the past, the museum's highly interactive displays make full use of the most modern technologies with lots of buttons to press and levers to pull. There is also a dedicated hands-on gallery – Xperiment! – full of science-related activities for kids to try out.

MUSEUM OF TRANSPORT, GLASGOW

LOCATION:
1 Bunhouse Road,
Kelvin Hall, Glasgow,
Lanarkshire G3 8DP
TEL: 0141 287 2720
OPENING TIMES:
10–5 Mon–Thur,
11–5 Fri & Sun
ADM: Free
GETTING THERE:
M8 J17 or 19, follow
signs from city centre
Underground: Kelvin
Hall
Train: Partick Station
FACILITIES:
Some on-site
parking, café,
souvenir shop
DISABLED:
Wheelchair access
(separate entrance)

DESPITE ITS DISTINCT lack of interactivity, this veritable temple of mechanised movement is now the most visited transport museum in the UK. Conventional wisdom has it that unless a museum is prepared to enliven its exhibits with hands-on games and snazzy audio-visuals, then the crowds will soon dry up. Somehow, this Glasgow attraction seems to have bucked the trend. Denied the chance to jump aboard and play with these vintage vehicles (or even see them set in motion), visitors are instead invited to appreciate the often-overlooked aesthetics of transport; to understand how these essentially functional machines have become over time some of the most enduring icons of the modern age. In many ways, the place feels more like an art gallery than a conventional museum – and visitors to art galleries don't usually complain because you're not allowed to prod the Rembrandts.

There are some concessions to modernity, including several arcade driving games (including a very good "test your reflexes" game designed to show the dangers of speeding), and you can explore a replica 1930s street scene and a reconstruction of Glasgow Underground Station. The real joy of this collection, however, comes simply from admiring the long lines of vehicles; the rows of trucks, trains, trams, railway locomotives, motorcycles, model boats and, of course, cars. Vintage, sporting, people carrier – every type of car is represented and many have tags displaying their original prices, allowing you to dream of picking up a Ferrari for less than £1000.

MUSEUM OF WELSH LIFE

LOCATION:
St Fagans,
Cardiff CF5 6XB
TEL: 0292 0573500
OPENING TIMES:
Jul–Sep: 10–6 daily;
Oct–Jun: 10–5 daily
ADM: Adult £5.30,
Child £3.20, Under
5's free, Family £14,
Conc's £3.90
GETTING THERE:
Road: M4 J33,
A4232
Train: Cardiff
Central station
FACILITIES: Free
car park, restaurant,
tea rooms
DISABLED:
Wheelchair access
to most areas (but
upper floors of
some cottages
inaccessible),
adapted toilets,
tactile maps for the
visually impaired,
disabled car
parking
WEBSITE: www.
nmgw.ac.uk

Croeso i Amgueddfa Werin Cymru, or Welcome to the Museum of Welsh Life. This is one of the largest openair museums in Europe. Spread across 100 acres of beautiful Glamorgan countryside are various re-created environments from the last 2,000 years of Welsh history.

The emphasis here is on interaction; you can pretend to be a time-traveller wending your way through the mud and thatch huts of a primitive Celtic village, tending to the animals in a 19th-century farmyard, learning your lessons in a Victorian schoolroom or doing the weekly shop in a 1920s' grocery. There are festivals, theatre performances, storytellings and craft demonstrations by black-

smiths, skilled wood turners and potters, as well as opportunities to try some of the crafts for yourself. Children in particular, are always eager to be let loose with a ball of clay and a potter's wheel. Afterwards you can take a ride in a horse-drawn carriage, travelling in style past the medieval farmhouse and Tudor Manor.

NATIONAL BOTANIC GARDEN OF WALES

LOCATION:
Middleton Hall,
Llanartne,
Carmathenshire
SA32 8HG

TEL: 01558 668 768

OPENING TIMES:
May–Aug: 10–6 daily,
Sep–Oct: 10–5.30
daily, Nov–Dec:
10–4.30 daily

ADM: Adult £6.50,
Child £3, Conc's £5,
Family £16

GETTING THERE:
Road: M4 (J49), then
A48, follow signs to
B4310
Train: Carmathen
Station (6 miles),
then bus

FACILITIES:
On-site parking,
café, shop

DISABLED:
Wheelchair access,
adapted toilets

WEBSITE: www.
gardenofwales.org.uk

OPENED TO MUCH fanfare in May 2000, the National Botanic Garden of Wales (or Gardd Fotaneg Genedlaethol Cymru in its native tongue) was the first national botanic garden to be built in Britain for over 200 years. It was a huge undertaking which saw a 568-acre previously derelict 18th-century estate transformed in a little over 10 years (and at a cost of some £45 million) into one of the most important, not to say impressive, collections of plants in Europe. Located in the lovely, temperate Towy Valley, its centrepiece is the appropriately named Great Glasshouse which, at over 100m long and 60m wide, is the largest single span glasshouse in the world. Designed by Sir Norman Foster, it's home to a spectacular array of tropical plants – there are representatives from Chile, California, Australia, South Africa and the Mediterranean – as well as an interactive exhibit, the "Bioverse", the aim of which is to allow visitors to see, feel and smell what it's like to be a plant. Surrounding this is a wonderful collection of botanic creations including a 220m-long herbaceous border made up of no less than 17,000 plants, and a Welsh Garden of native meadows and forest. There's also an Aquatic Ecology Laboratory, an Insectarium, an Energy Centre – as supremely ecologically friendly as you'd expect, the garden produces all its own energy – and an open area, Middleton Square, in which concerts and theatre productions are held in summer.

NATIONAL GALLERY

LOCATION: Trafalgar Square, London WC2N 5DN
TEL: 020 7747 2885
OPENING TIMES: 10–6 Mon–Sat, 2–6 Sun
ADM: Free, charges apply for some temporary exhibitions
GETTING THERE: Underground: Charing Cross, Leicester Square, Embankment
Bus: 3, 6, 9, 11, 12, 13, 15, 23, 24, 29, 53, 88, 91, 109, 139, 159, 176, 184, 196
FACILITIES: Gift shop, café, restaurant
DISABLED: Wheelchair access, Loop system for hard of hearing
WEBSITE: www.national-gallery.org.uk

NATIONAL PORTRAIT GALLERY

LOCATION: St Martin's Place, London WC2H 0HE
TEL: 020 7306 0055
OPENING TIMES: As above
ADM: As above
GETTING THERE: Underground: As above
Bus: As above
FACILITIES: Restaurant, café, shop, audio tour available
DISABLED: Wheelchair access
WEBSITE: www.npg.org.uk

ON TRAFALGAR SQUARE facing Nelson's Column, in the heart of the capital, this collection of some 2,000-plus pictures is one of the country's most splendid national treasures. All the greats from the history of western European painting are here: Cézanne, Constable, Leonardo da Vinci, Monet, Picasso, Raphael, Rembrandt, Rubens, Titian, Turner, Van Eyck, Van Gogh... the list is endless. It has been internationally acclaimed as one of the world's great art galleries and yet has attracted its fair share of controversy. When it opened in 1838, the building was widely criticised for its lack of grace and symmetry. This was nothing, however, to the furore aroused by the proposed Sainsbury's extension in the early 1980s. The original glass and steel design was described by Prince Charles as a "monstrous carbuncle" and was promptly dropped for the more traditional, conservative design we see today.

NATIONAL PORTRAIT GALLERY

If history is, as Thomas Carlyle once claimed, merely the 'biographies of great men', then the National Portrait Gallery is its picture album. Arranged in chronological order from the 13th century (top floor) to the present day (ground floor) are 2,000 pictures of Britain's greatest national figures – kings, queens, statesmen, politicians, scientists and writers – rendered in a variety of styles. The collection includes Holbein's wonderful Renaissance portraits of Henrys VII and VIII, a cubist T.S. Eliot by Jacob Epstein and Annigoni's famous film-star treatment of Elizabeth II.

NATIONAL MUSEUM OF PHOTOGRAPHY, FILM & T.V.

LOCATION:
Pictureville,
Bradford, West
Yorkshire BO1 1NQ
TEL: 01274 202 030
OPENING TIMES:
10–6 Tues–Sun &
Bank Hol Mon
ADM: Free, IMAX:
Adult £5.80, Child &
Conc's £4
GETTING THERE:
Road: M62 J26, then
M606
Train: Bradford
Interchange Station
(5-minute walk),
Bradford Forster
Square Station
(10-minute walk)
FACILITIES:
Café, shop
DISABLED:
Wheelchair access,
audio & braille
guides available,
adapted toilets,
disabled parking
spaces available
WEBSITE: www.
nmpft.org.uk

FROM SHADOWY IMAGES on light-sensitive paper to the latest pixillated digital animation, this recently revamped museum traces the long and fascinating history of the captured image. There are 6 floors to explore, starting with an exhibition on 19th-century cameras (you'll leave with a new found appreciation of your APS system, getting these cumbersome beasts to capture a single simple black and white image was a painstakingly long and complicated process) and finishing on the top floor with a look at that most modern of media, TV advertising. In between is a mountain of exhibits showing how the camera – both moving and still – has become, over the last 150 years, the most powerful communicative tool in the world. Every possible aspect of screen technology is covered – photography, animation, feature films, special effects, digital TV – and its historic and social implications explored. The sheer range of exhibits means that there will be something here to capture the interest of every member of the family. Parents can revel in the nostalgia of TV Heaven as they sit in a private booth watching a constant stream of vintage TV classics while children sample some of the museum's more hi-tech interactive offerings – they can try their hand at newsreading, learn to operate a TV camera or discover the secrets of bluescreen technology as they "fly" on a magic carpet. And, once you've had your fill of exploring, you could always settle back and watch a classic film or a state-of-the-art IMAX presentation at one of the museum's three cinemas.

NATIONAL MUSEUM OF SCOTLAND

LOCATION:
Chambers Street,
Edinburgh EH1 1JF
TEL: 0131 247 4422
OPENING TIMES:
10–5 Mon–Sat,
12-5 Sun, late night
opening Tues until
8pm
ADM: Adult £3, Child
free, Conc's £1.50
(ticket includes entry
to Royal Museum of
Scotland), free entry
Tues 4.30–8pm
GETTING THERE:
Road: A1, A703
Train: Waverley
station
Bus: Most buses
from Prince's Street
go past the museum
FACILITIES: Museum
shop, 2 restaurants
and a café. Guided
tours available
DISABLED:
Wheelchair access
to all parts of
museum, adapted
toilets
WEBSITE: www.
nms.ac.uk

OPENED BY THE Queen on 1 December 1998, this is the only museum in Scotland devoted to the history of Scotland itself. The six sections within this beautiful, specially constructed sandstone building tell the story of Scotland and the Scottish people from pre-history to the present day; from volcano-rav-aged landscape to industrial power. It contains some of the country's most precious artifacts, including the Monymusk Reliquary, a tiny shrine made in around AD 750 containing the relics of St Columba, which was carried into battle at the head of Robert the Bruce's army at the Battle of Bannockburn. There's also a brooch belonging to Mary Queen of Scots, James VI's stirrup cup and Bonnie Prince Charlie's canteen. Perhaps the most impressive exhibits, however, are those relating to Scotland's Industrial Revolution – in particular, the vast, 40ft-high, iron and wood Newcombe Atmospheric Engine, one of the world's first steam engines, which seems to dominate the entire museum.

The exhibits on display in the Twentieth Century Gallery have been chosen in a particularly novel way. Rather than rely on the whims of curators and administrators, the gallery asked members of the public, as well as political and national figures, to nominate those items which, for them, best represented the 20th century. The 800 exhibits make a strange and eclectic display. There's a washing machine, a typewriter, a video game player, a packet of contraceptive pills, an NHS card and, of course, a bottle of Irn Bru "made in Scotland, from girders".

NATIONAL RAILWAY MUSEUM

LOCATION:
Leeman Road,
York YO26 4XJ
TEL: 01904 621 261
OPENING TIMES:
10–6 daily
ADM: Adult £6.50,
Child Free,
Conc's £4.40

This is the largest railway museum in the world with artifacts, memorabilia and rolling stock from throughout the entire railway age — from Stephenson's Rocket to the Eurostar. Its pride and joy, however, is its huge collection of classic steam engines arranged in a star pattern around a 1955 turntable in the Great Hall. You can go inside most, including the Mallard, the fastest steam loco-

GETTING THERE:
Road: A59, A64,
A1079, then
signposted from
York's ring road
Train: York station
is 500yds away
Bus: Special bus
service runs from
York Minster every
30 mins Apr–Oct,
call no. above for
details
FACILITIES: Long stay
parking available on-
site (charges apply),
gift shop, restaurant,
café, barbecue dur-
ing summer, refer-
ence library
DISABLED:
Wheelchair access
to most parts of the
museum, wheelchair
loan available,
special parking at
the City entrance
WEBSITE: www.
nrm.org.uk

motive in the world capable of travelling at speeds of up to 125mph.

The nearby Station Hall is filled with an equally impressive array of vintage carriages including several once owned by the Royal Family. At the "Palace on Wheels" exhibition, you can see the privations that train-travelling royals have had to endure over the years – sumptuous bedrooms, fabulously appointed reading rooms and salons, not to mention Queen Victoria's gold plated toilet. The Queen, it seemed, never fully embraced the capabilities of the new technology and would not allow her train to travel above 40mph.

Children are well catered for with Play 'n' Picnic areas, an interactive learning centre where they can sort letters and learn about the construction of the Channel Tunnel, a large model railway as well as regular visits from Thomas the Tank Engine.

A new £4 million wing, "The Work", has just opened containing a locomotive workshop where visitors can watch trains being restored from a viewing gallery.

THE NATURAL HISTORY MUSEUM

LOCATION:
Cromwell Road,
London SW7 5BD
TEL: 020 7942 5000
OPENING TIMES:
10–5.50 Mon–Sat,
11–5.50 Sun
ADM: Adult £6.50,
Child Free, Conc's
£3.50, Free entry to
all after 4.30pm
Mon–Fri and after
5pm Sat, Sun &
Bank Holidays

AS EVERY CHILD knows, the Natural History Museum means dinosaurs. These 65-million-year-old attractions have always been the museum's biggest draw. Until recently, the nation's youth was happy to marvel at fossils in cases and plaster cast reconstructions, particularly the enormous diplodocus in the vast cathedral-like central hall. In the wake of the worldwide success of *Jurassic Park*, however, the dinosaur section was revamped and now features a rather gruesome (and thus extremely popular) animatronic display, as well as an illuminated walkway taking you past models and interactive displays.

GETTING THERE:
Underground:
South Kensington
Bus: 14, 49, 70,
345, C1
FACILITIES:
Restaurant, café,
coffee bar, snack
bar, gallery shop,
bookshop, souvenir
and gift shop, baby-changing facilities
DISABLED:
Wheelchair access,
adapted toilets
WEBSITE: www.
nhm.ac.uk

Although children often forget it, the Natural History Museum does have more to offer besides monsters from the past. It is divided into two sections, the Life Galleries and the Earth Galleries. Highlights from the Life Galleries include a section cut from a 1,300-year-old giant sequoia tree and an awesome life-size model of a blue whale suspended from the Mammal Gallery ceiling. The Earth Galleries are reached via an escalator which ascends into a suspended metallic globe. Here you can experience a virtual earthquake in a reconstructed Japanese supermarket and see the eerie lava casts of people killed as they attempted to flee the Pompeii volcanic eruption in the 1st century AD.

These days the museum is very keen on promoting interaction; with lots of buttons to press, levers to pull and videos to see. Nonetheless, it still remains one of the best places in the country to simply stand and marvel.

NORTH YORKSHIRE MOORS RAILWAY

LOCATION:
Pickering Station, Pickering, North Yorkshire YO18 7AJ
TEL: 01751 472 508
OPENING TIMES:
Late Mar–Oct: daily
ADM:
Adult £8.90, Child £4.50, Conc's £7.50
GETTING THERE:
Road: Pickering Station is on the A170 between Scarborough and Thirsk
Train: Mainline service to Grosmont from Whitby and Middlesbrough
FACILITIES:
Car parks at Pickering, Levisham, Goathland and Grosmont stations, refreshments and shops at Pickering, Goathland and Grosmont
WEBSITE: www. nymr.demon.co.uk

There are few more enjoyable ways to see the North Yorkshire countryside than aboard a gently puffing steam train, chugging your way past moors and forests. This beautifully preserved railway takes you on a scenic 18 mile journey between the medieval town of Pickering, where a lively market is held every Monday, and Grosmont, passing through Levisham, the gateway to Newton Dale with its stunning glacial valley, and Goathland, the scenic rural village featured in TV's Heartbeat, on the way.

The railway has more to offer, however, than mere scenic views. Formerly part of the Midland and Great Northern Joint Railway laid out by the great rail pioneer George Stephenson, it is also an important historical artefact and has been run as a living museum since 1974. At Grosmont, the operational headquarters, you can view a wide range of vintage locomotives, including the much loved 1943 Vera Lynn, displayed in its engine shed. Various special events take place throughout the year including a Thomas the Tank Engine weekend, a vintage car weekend and brass band concerts in the Levisham Station paddock.

Steam enthusiasts looking to fulfill that childhood dream should sign up for one of the railway's 'Footplate Awareness' courses when they will be shown how to operate one of the mighty engines.

OSBORNE HOUSE

LOCATION:
York Avenue, East Cowes, Isle of Wight PO32 6JY

TEL: 01983 200 022

OPENING TIMES:
Apr–Sep 10–5,
Oct 10–4

ADM:
Adult £6.90, Child £3.50, Conc's £5.20, Family £17.50

GETTING THERE:
Road: It's off the A3021
Train: Ryde Esplanade Station (7 miles away), then bus

FACILITIES:
On-site parking, tea-room, café, souvenir shop, guided tours

DISABLED:
Wheelchair access to ground floor and gardens only

WEBSITE: www.english-heritage.org.uk

OF ALL BRITAIN'S many royal palaces, Osborne House on the Isle of Wight was the one held in the most affection by Queen Victoria, who spent her final days here in 1901. Built during her reign, in an Italianate style according to a design drawn up by her beloved husband, Albert, its apartments have been carefully restored to look much as they would have done during their 19th- century heyday. Though ornate and, as you would expect, beautifully furnished, the house has a distinctly sombre quality to it. Following Albert's death in 1861 the Queen remained in mourning for the rest of her life and Osborne's rooms are littered with reminders of her grief – you can see Albert's personal bathroom preserved just as he left it, a specially commissioned portrait of the Prince Consort which sat by the Queen's bed, and a starkly melancholic study of the Queen herself entitled "The Queen Called Sorrow" by Landseer. In parts, the house feels a little like an informal mausoleum, although it does have its more lighthearted exhibits, including the billiard room where the Queen used to challenge her ladies in waiting to games, and a room filled with furniture entirely made from antlers. The most charming part of the whole estate, however, is undoubtedly the delightful Swiss Cottage, also designed by Albert, and the nearby royal children's play area which has a toy fort and a miniature kitchen. Both of these can be reached from the house aboard a wonderfully grand horse-drawn carriage.

PLEASURE BEACH, GREAT YARMOUTH

LOCATION: South Beach Parade, Great Yarmouth NR30 3EH
TEL: 01493 844 585
OPENING TIMES: Mar–Sept, dates and times vary.
ADM: Free entry; rides can be paid for either with tokens, 50p each or wristbands £8
GETTING THERE: Road: From South: M11 J6, A11, A14, A143, A146. From North: A17, A47, A12. Train: Great Yarmouth station Bus: First Blue Service from Norwich
FACILITIES: Sweet shops, inn, tea room
DISABLED: Most rides accessible, adapted toilets
WEBSITE: www. pleasure-beach. co.uk

THIS NINE-ACRE sea-front site, encompassing over 70 rides, is East Anglia's most popular tourist attraction. Its flagship ride, the Ejector Seat, is an ingenious variation on the traditional bungee jump. Passengers start the ride at ground level in a tethered two-seater cage. Once released, the "mother of all elastic bands" flings its victims into the air to a height of 160ft, going from 0–70mph in just under a second, before returning them back down to earth at 125mph. Alternatively, there's the Terminator or Top Spin, a large 360° spinning gondola which can terrify a staggering 900 people an hour, or Sheer Terror, a walk-through attraction where performing arts students from Great Yarmouth College dress up in scary costumes (mad axeman, Hannibal Lecter etc.) and try to terrify anyone who enters. There's also a go-cart track, a log flume, a waltzer, and an adventure golf course, as well as various rollercoasters.

Great Yarmouth developed into a popular seaside resort between 1800 and 1860, and the seafront centre was born in 1909. The original Pleasure Beach had a scenic railway and little else until, in 1911, it acquired a Joywheel; its collection of attractions has been expanding ever since. A reminder of this earlier, gentler era is provided by Gallopers, a merry-go-round built in 1915, still with its original hand-carved horses.

PLEASURELAND, SOUTHPORT

LOCATION:
Marine Drive,
Southport PR8 1RX
TEL: 01704 532717
OPENING TIMES:
Mar–early Nov week-
ends only; open
daily during school
holidays. Hours of
opening vary–call in
advance
ADM: Free entry;
wristband for 10
rides Adult £12.99,
Child £7.50,
Under 1.2m £5,
Family £36
GETTING THERE:
By car: From north:
M6 J31, follow A59
through Preston,
take A565 and follow
signs. From south:
M6 J26 onto M58,
exit J3 onto A570,
follow signs
Parking: Ample car
and coach parking
facilities; charges
apply
Train: Southport
station
Bus: A shuttle
operates during the
summer between
Southport Station
and Pleasureland,
Stagecoach service
no.X59 also stops at
the park
FACILITIES:
Restaurants and gift
shops.
DISABLED:
Wheelchair access,
adapted toilets,
access to rides at
the discretion of
the park.
WEBSITE: www.
pleasureland.uk.com

Previously the epitome of the old fashioned leisure park, full of gentle rides and rickety old rollercoasters, Pleasureland has, in recent years, been running fast to catch up with its better known rivals. Its current pride and joy is the Traumatizer, the tallest, fastest, all-round nastiest suspension rollercoaster in the country which takes its passengers on a hair-raising journey through loops, corkscrews, rolls, inversions and flipovers. Opened in 1999, it has proved a fitting successor to the park's previous showpiece, the Cyclone, a wooden rollercoaster which first saw action way back in 1937 (but which was still thrilling enough in 1996 to be voted the 3rd best rollercoaster in Europe by a group of American coaster afficianados).

Despite its revamp, Pleasureland remains at heart a deeply traditional establishment that manages to keep its visitors in touch with the spirit of fairgrounds past. You can take a trip down memory lane aboard the 1954 Gulliver Carousel, the 1923 River Boat Journey and (one of the real grand old men of British funparks) a 1914 rollercoaster — don't panic, it was fully renovated in 1996.

The park also contains a several water rides, three go-kart tracks and the "Sultan Towers", a children's play area with a bouncy castle, mini rollercoaster and junior Ferris wheel.

ROCK CIRCUS

LOCATION:
The London Pavilion,
1 Piccadilly Circus,
London W1V 9LA
TEL: 020 7734 7203
OPENING TIMES: 11–9
11–9 Mon, Wed,
Thurs, Sun; 11–10
Fri–Sat; 12–9 Tues
ADM: Adult £8.25,
Child £6.25, Conc's
£6.95

GETTING THERE:
Underground:
Piccadilly Circus
Bus: 3, 6, 9, 12,
13, 14, 15, 19, 22,
23, 38, 53, 88, 94,
139, 159
FACILITIES:
Rock & pop shop,
hot snacks,
sweets bar
DISABLED:
Adapted toilets
WEBSITE: www.
rock-circus.com

THREE FLOORS OF designer doppelgängers sing you through the history of popular music. In the New Music Revolving Show, in Europe's largest revolving auditorium, animatronic stars from Michael Jackson to the Spice Girls belt out their biggest hits – the sound is relayed through individual infra-red head-sets. There's also a horde of priceless rock memorabilia, including a shirt that once belonged to Elvis Presley and the jacket worn by Ringo Starr in *A Hard Day's Night,* as well as various signed gold and platinum records.

ROMAN BATHS & PUMP ROOM

LOCATION:
Stall Street,
Bath, BA1 1LZ
TEL: 01225 477 785
OPENING TIMES:
Apr–Sept 9–6 daily
(also, 8pm–10pm in
Aug); Oct–Mar:
9.30–5 Mon–Sat,
10.30–5 Sun
ADM: £6.90, Child £4,
Family £17.50

H ERE IN BATH you will find an elegant 18th-century tearoom built over some of the best-preserved Roman remains in Britain. In AD 75 the Romans erected a small shrine to the Goddess Sulis Minerva next to a natural hot spring, where pilgrims would come to worship and throw curses written on sheets of lead into the sacred water. Inveterate bathers that they were, however, the Romans soon put the water to less spiritual use at a huge bathing complex where the great and good of Roman society would go to socialise, chat about the day's business and, of course, bathe.

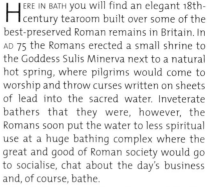

The baths were only rediscovered in the 18th century when the prevailing health fashion for "taking the waters" led to a new spate of construction near the spring. Remarkably, the baths had remained largely intact. Indeed, the Great Bath still receives its daily water from pipes laid down by the Romans. In summer, at night, the complex is beautifully floodlit.

GETTING THERE:
Road: M4, then A4
Train: Bath station
FACILITIES: Free
audio tour of baths;
museum, gift shop,
restaurant and
coffee room in Pump
Room, glass of
spring water 45p
DISABLED: No wheel-chair access to
Baths, Pump Room
is fully accessible
WEBSITE: www.
romanbaths.

The Pump Room, an exquisitely tasteful tea and coffee house, fulfilled much the same function for the 18th-century social élite as the baths had done for their Roman fore-bears. It was primarily a meeting place, somewhere to see and be seen, as described in the novels of Jane Austen. Today visitors to the Pump Room can enjoy a traditional pot of tea or sample a glass of spa water from the pump fountain. The spring still produces 250,000 gallons of water a day at a tempera-ture of 45.6°C or 116°F.

ROYAL ACADEMY OF ARTS

LOCATION: Piccadilly, London W1V 0DS
TEL: 020 7300 8000
ADM: Prices vary per exhibition, usually between £3–£9
OPENING TIMES: Daily 10–6, late night Friday until 8.30pm; individual exhibition times vary
GETTING THERE: Underground: Piccadilly Circus, Green Park
Bus: 9, 14, 19, 22, 38 stop at the Academy's gate, 3, 6, 12, 13, 88, 159 stop at Piccadilly Circus
FACILITIES: Restaurant, café, shop
DISABLED: Wheelchair access to all areas, wheelchair hire available in advance
WEBSITE: www.royalacademy.org.uk

THE ROYAL ACADEMY of Arts was founded by George III in 1768 and was the first institution in Britain to be devoted solely to the promotion of the visual arts. It's unique in that it is governed and run by artists rather than academics or government appointees. The list of former Royal Academicians reads like a Who's Who of British art – Sir Joshua Reynolds, Constable, Gainsborough, Turner and Stanley Spencer among them – all of whom have donated work to the Academy's permanent exhibition. Current members of the academy include Peter Blake and David Hockney.

The great joy of the Royal Academy is that you are guaranteed to see something different every time you visit as most of the gallery space is devoted to loan and temporary exhibitions. The upcoming programme will include exhibitions of Turner watercolours, Botticelli drawings (for Dante's Divine Comedy), Rembrandt's women, French painting from Ingres to Matisse, as well, of course, as the famous Summer Exhibition.

ROYAL BOTANIC GARDENS EDINBURGH

LOCATION:
Inverleith Row,
Edinburgh,
Midlothian EH3 5LR
TEL: 0131 552 7171
OPENING TIMES:
Feb & Oct: 9.30–5
daily, Mar & Sep:
9.30–6 daily,
Apr–Aug: 9.30–7
daily, Nov–Jan:
9.30–4 daily
ADM: Free
GETTING THERE:
Road: Off the A902
1 mile north of
Edinburgh city
centre
Bus: No.s 23, 27, 37
Train: Waverley
Station
FACILITIES:
Café, bar, souvenir
shop
DISABLED:
Wheelchair access
WEBSITE: www.
rbge.org.uk

SCOTLAND'S PREMIER BOTANIC institute began life as a small physic garden at Holyrood in 1670 before being transplanted to its present location to the north of Edinburgh city centre in the early 19th century, since when it has grown into one of the UK's most important collections of plants. The site encompasses some 70 acres of landscaped gardens divided into numerous themed areas: an ecological garden decorated with native Scottish plants; a world-famous rock garden full of sub-arctic vegetation; a winter garden laid out with snowdrops and witch hazel and a Chinese garden full of tiny, delicate oriental plants and a charming mini-pagoda. The gardens' undoubted highlights, however, are the magnificent 19th-century hot houses (including the country's tallest palm house), full of lush, dense, tropical vegetation.

Home to the largest rhododendron collection in the country, the gardens are a riot of colour in summer with miles of marked walks taking you past the flower beds, rare trees (all carefully labelled) and enormous, winding herbaceous border. There's also a hands-on exhibition hall, a particular favourite with children, with interactive displays, microscopes and a constantly changing programme of temporary art exhibitions.

ROYAL MUSEUM OF SCOTLAND

LOCATION:
Chambers Street,
Edinburgh EH1 1JF
TEL: 0131 225 7534
OPENING TIMES:
10–5 Mon, Wed–Sat,
10–8 Tues, 12–5 Sun
ADM: Adults £3,
Child free,
Conc's £1.50
(ticket includes entry
to National Museum
of Scotland); free
entry on Tues 4.30–8
GETTING THERE:
Road: A1, A703
Train: Waverley
station
Bus: Most buses
from Princes Street
go past the museum
FACILITIES: Café and
tearoom, museum
shop, free guided
tours, metered
parking in streets
around the museum
DISABLED: Museum
is fully accessible
with lifts to all floors
and adapted toilets
WEBSITE: www.
nms.ac.uk

O**N CHAMBERS STREET**, by the memorial to Greyfriars Bobby, stands the Royal Museum of Scotland which, along with the new National Museum of Scotland next door, represents Edinburgh's answer to London's Kensington museum complex. There's a wonderfully eclectic range of exhibits on display in this Crystal Palace-like iron and glass building, including some exquisite French silverware from the reign of Louis XIV; ceramics from ancient Greece, sculptures from Rome and Assyria, and even a native American totem pole. There's also an interactive technology section where, in amongst the steam behemoths of industrial Britain, you can find the 1896 Hawk Glider, Britain's first flying machine. There are also sections devoted to oriental art, geology, fossils, ethnology and natural history – the last a veritable temple to taxidermy with cases and cases full of stuffed animals and birds.

ROYAL YACHT BRITANNIA

LOCATION:
Leith Docks, Leith,
Edinburgh EH6 6JJ
TEL: 0131 555 5566
OPENING TIMES:
10–4.30 Summer,
10–3.30 Winter
ADM:
Apr–Sep: Adult £7,
Child & Conc's £3.25,
Oct–Mar: Adult
£6.75, Child £3,
Conc's £2.75

IN 1953, THE recently crowned Queen Elizabeth II found herself the proud possessor of a brand new floating palace. Built in the Clyde shipyards, the vast yacht would spend the next four decades transporting the Queen and her royal retinue all over the globe, its glittering interior providing the setting for innumerable state banquets and functions (plus the odd private family shindig). Primarily responsible for the design and decor of the ship's interior, the royal couple always counted it among their favourite residences – after all, it's one thing to inherit a

GETTING THERE:
Road: M8, A1, A70,
A71, A9, follow
brown & white
tourist signs from
the city centre
Train: Waverley
Station, then X30
bus
FACILITIES:
Café, souvenir shop
DISABLED:
Limited wheelchair
access

palace, quite another to have it built to your own specifications. As a final, symbolic act before decommissioning, it was given the honour of sailing the last British dignitaries away from China following the handover of Hong Kong.

Finally deemed surplus to royal requirements after nearly half a century of active service, this stately galleon has returned to the country of its birth where it can be visited for the first time by the hoi polloi. In the company of an audio guide you can tour its gleaming decks to see the Dining Room – its huge tables laid out as if for a state banquet – kitchens, engine room, private apartments (including the Queen's own bedroom) and watch films detailing the history of the ship and showing some of the scores of world leaders – Winston Churchill, Boris Yeltsin, Ronald Reagan and Margaret Thatcher among them – to have enjoyed its special brand of marine hospitality. The Royal Launch, which was used to bring these dignitaries from shore to yacht is also on display.

SALISBURY CATHEDRAL

LOCATION:
The Close, Salisbury,
Wiltshire SP1 2EJ
TEL: 01722 555 120
OPENING TIMES:
Jun–Aug: 7am–8pm
daily, Sep–May:
7am–6.30pm daily
ADM: Free, suggest-
ed donations: Adult
£3, Child £1, Family
£6, Conc's £2
GETTING THERE:
Road: Off the A30,
follow the signs from
Salisbury ring road
Train: Salisbury
Station, 5-minute
walk away
FACILITIES:
On-site parking
(£5 per car), coffee
shop, souvenir shop
DISABLED:
Wheelchair access
to ground floor only
WEBSITE: www.
salisburycathedral.
org.uk

OWING TO THE sheer speed of its construc-tion, Salisbury's great medieval cathe-dral is one of only a handful in the entire country to display a single cohesive architec-tural style, in this instance English Gothic. It was built during the 13th century in a mere 38 years (38 years may not seem that mere, but by medieval standards it was practically light speed; most cathedrals took well over 100 years to complete) although the spire, which at 123m is the tallest in the country, wasn't added until early in the next century. As the original design didn't include a spire, its addition caused some major architectur-al problems. It weighs a mighty 6,400 tonnes and, if you look closely at the stone pillars supporting it, you can see that they have become bent under the enormous weight. The interior is light and airy, with huge windows overlooking the nave, and is lined with sculpted tombs of medieval cru-sader heroes. The clock in the North Aisle, which was built in 1386, is the oldest contin-uously working timepiece in the world and stands in stark contrast to some of the more recent additions to the cathedral's interior, most notably the revolving glass prism etched with an image of the cathedral. Also, look out for the model of the cathedral in the north transept, surrounded by miniature blacksmiths, carpenters and masons.

The cathedral's cloisters are the largest in the country and contain some wonderful bas relief friezes depicting early Biblical stories as well as one of only four surviving copies of the Magna Carta.

SCIENCE MUSEUM

LOCATION:
Exhibition Road,
London SW7 2DD
TEL: 020 7938 8008
OPENING TIMES:
10–6 daily
ADM: Adult £6.50,
Child £3.50, Conc's
£3.50; free entry to
all after 4.30pm
GETTING THERE:
Underground:
South Kensington
Bus: 9, 10, 14, 49,
52, 74, 345, C1
FACILITIES:
Museum shop,
bookshop, post
office, Bureau de
Change, cash
machine

Children's affection for this collection of whirring gizmos and gadgets is such that the museum has recently started letting them spend the night. At these evening campnights, mini science nuts are treated to an after-hours tour of the building, workshops and bedtime stories. The rest of the population, who must visit this most entertaining of museums in the daylight, can only look on with envy.

On the ground floor, dedicated to industrial and technological progress, you will find steam engines (including Stephenson's "Puffing Billy"), a model reworking of Foucault's Pendulum (the device which first illustrated the turning of the earth), a World War II V2 rocket and the Apollo 10 space capsule. The Launch Pad, on the first floor, is full of flashing, beeping interactive displays and, as a result, is permanently inhabited by throngs of wide-eyed kids. Adults wearing a similar expression can be found in the

DISABLED:
An "Access and
Facilities Guide" is
available. Disabled
Person's Enquiry
Line 020 7938 9788
WEBSITE: www.
nmsi.ac.uk

Science of Sport gallery, where pride of place is given to a £2 million Formula 1 McLaren.

In 2000 the museum opened a new £47 million 10,000 square metre Welcome Wing, which has increased the available floor area of the museum by a third. Dedicated to explaining the most modern of scientific and technological breakthroughs, it holds an IMAX (large screen) 3D film theatre as well as exhibitions on the internet and genetic engineering..

Location: The Mound, Edinburgh EH2 2EL
Tel: 0131 624 6200
Opening Times: Mon–Sat 10–5, Sun 2–5
Adm: Free, charges may apply for temporary exhibitions
Getting there:
Road: M8, A1, A70, A71, A90
Train: Waverley Station
Facilities: Café, shop
Disabled: Wheelchair access to most of the gallery apart from gallery A1; adapted toilets
Website: www.nat-galscot.ac.uk

Scotland's pre-eminent art collection is housed in a handsome neo-classical building designed by William Henry Playfair (17890–1857) with its foundations being laid in 1850 by Prince Albert. Inside, you'll find works by Old Masters — Cézanne, Constable, Gauguin, Monet, Poussin, Raphael, Renoir, Rubens, Titian, Turner, Velasquez, Van Gogh et al — hanging alongside paintings by native artists such as Ramsay, Raeburn and McTaggert. The most famous picture in the collection is probably Botticelli's Madonna and Child (1480) which the gallery bought (with a little help from the lottery commission) for a cool £20 million.

SOTTISH NATIONAL PORTRAIT GALLERY
The Scottish National Portrait Gallery is filled with images of the men and women who, since the 16th century, have done most to shape the country's history and ideology — monarchs, soldiers, writers, philosophers, industrialists, poets, criminals...the list goes on. Obviously, as the portraits have been chosen on the basis of identity rather than ability, the quality of the work does vary enormously, but there are, nonetheless, many fine works on display.

Within The National Galleries of Scotland there is: Scottish National Gallery of Modern Art at Belford Road where there is an outstanding collection of 20th-century paintings, sculpture and graphic art. Includes major works by Bacon, Baselitz, Bonnard, Hockney, Moore, Matisse and Picasso.
Dean Gallery also at Belford Road which opened in 1999 and provides a home for the Eduardo Paolozzi gift of sculpture and graphic art. There is also a major library and archive centre.

SHAKESPEARE'S GLOBE

LOCATION:
Bear Gardens, New Globe Walk, Bankside, London SE1 9DT

TEL: 020 7902 1500

OPENING TIMES:
10–5 daily, for performance times call in advance

ADM:
Museum: Adult £7.50, Child £5, Family £23, Conc's £6, for performance prices call in advance

GETTING THERE:
Underground: London Bridge
Bus: No.s 17, 95, 149, 184

FACILITIES:
Café, licensed restaurant, souvenir shop, guided tour

DISABLED:
Limited wheelchair access

WEBSITE:
www.shakespeare-globe.org

THE GLOBE IS a perfect modern recreation of the Elizabethan theatre where many of Shakespeare's plays were premiered, including Othello, Macbeth and Romeo & Juliet. The original theatre burnt down in 1613 when an errant ember from a cannon (fired to let theatre goers know that the performance was about to begin) set the thatched roof alight. Demolished and forgotten about for the next 370 years, it was rebuilt a few hundred yards from its original location in the early 1990s. With its curved thatched roof (the first to grace a London building since the Great Fire of London) and wooden O-shaped auditorium, it is as historically accurate as modern safety standards will allow.

It is important to remember that theatregoing in Shakespeare's time was a much less refined activity than today. Back then, Bankside was the city's red light district, a messy agglomeration of brothels and drinking dens where people came to indulge in bawdy, rowdy entertainments such as gambling, bear-baiting and, of course, going to the theatre. There would have been no plush, padded seats in the old Globe and, consequently, you'll find none in the new. Rather, you have the choice of sitting on hard, wooden benches (although you can hire cushions) or standing in the open area in front of the stage, which is what the poorer theatre goers would have done in Shakespeare's day. Despite these hardships, it's great fun seeing the plays performed as they were originally intended and, even when there are no plays showing, you can still take a guided tour of the theatre and visit the multimedia exhibition which explains its long history.

THE SHAKESPEARE HOUSES

LOCATION: The Shakespeare Centre, Henley Street, Stratford-upon-Avon CV37 6QW
TEL: 01789 204 016
OPENING TIMES: Times vary per house and according to season, but usually open daily between 9.30/10–4/5
ADM: Joint ticket for all 5 houses £12, otherwise each house £5
GETTING THERE: Call no. above for details of individual houses

THE SHAKESPEARE HOUSES is a tour around the five buildings in Stratford-upon-Avon where the bard spent much of his early and later life. He was born in 1562 in a small house on Henley Street, where today you can find some beautiful period furniture and a small interactive display on his life. Nearby, at the home of his mother, Mary Arden, there are daily falconry displays. In 1582 the 20-year-old William married Anne Hathaway, the daughter of a local farmer. Her house, the next on the tour, is a beautifully preserved thatched Tudor farmhouse. Soon after, he moved to London, where his plays enjoyed such success that, by the time he returned to Stratford in 1611, he was the shareholder in a new theatre, the Globe, on the south bank of the River Thames, and had been granted royal patronage by James I. With his new-found wealth he

FACILITIES: Teashops at Mary Arden and Hall's Croft
DISABLED: Wheelchair access to Hall's Croft only
WEBSITE: www.shakespeare.org.uk

bought New Place, one of the largest houses in Stratford, where he would spend his final years. It was destroyed in the 18th century although the Elizabethan knot garden remains. He also spent much of his later life at Hall's Croft, a lovely gabled property and the home of Dr John Hall, who married Shakespeare's daughter.

SNOWDONIA NATIONAL PARK

SNOWDONIA NATIONAL PARK
LOCATION: National Park Office, Penrhydendraeth, Gwynedd LL48 6LP
TEL: 01766 770 274
GETTING THERE: Road: A55, A470, A487, A5, A494, A458
Train: Harlech, Barmouth, Betws-y-Coed, Bangor, Llanfayrfechan stations
FACILITIES: Many visitor centres (some village shops and post offices operate as tourist information points, recognisable from blue 'i' logo)
DISABLED: No specific facilities

HARLECH CASTLE
LOCATION: Castle Square, Harlech, Gwynedd LL46 2YH
TEL: 01766 780 552
OPENING TIMES: April–Oct: 9.30–6.30 daily, Nov–Mar: 9.30–4 Mon–Sat, 11–4 Sun
ADM: Adult £3, Child & Conc's £2, Family £8
GETTING THERE: Road: A496
Train: Barmouth, Port Madoc stations
FACILITIES: Limited parking, souvenir shop
DISABLED: No wheelchair access

SNOWDON MOUNTAIN RAILWAY
LOCATION: llanberis
TEL: 01286 870 223
OPERATING TIMES: Mar–Oct: daily

THE SNOWDONIA NATIONAL PARK covers an area of 840 square miles in northwest Wales, a vast swathe of countryside made up of myriad different landscapes: woodlands of ash, oak and hazel, steep glacial valleys, waterfalls and lakes – including Llyn Tegid, Wales's largest freshwater lake, which, according to local legends, was either formed when the keeper of Gaver's Well forgot to replace the lid one night, or was the result of a flood sent to punish a cruel local ruler. Rowing boats, sailboards and fishing permits are available from the lake warden. This is a walker's paradise with literally hundreds of well marked routes of varying degrees of difficulty – some more or less flat, others practically vertical. There are castles, such as the beautifully preserved 13th-century Harlech, with its

commanding views over Cardigan Bay and Caernarfon (*see* p.22), manor houses, farmhouses and cottages as well as caravan and picnic sites. The whole area is brimming with wildlife, including fish, wildfowl and otters. In fact, there are more nature reserves in Snowdonia than in any other national park in Britain. The park is also home, of course, to the snow-capped splendour of Mount Snowdon which, at 3,560ft, is the tallest peak in England or Wales. A steam railway chugs its way from Llanberis to the summit in a little under two-and-a-half hours, where you can take refreshment in the café and bar, write a postcard and pop it into the highest postbox in the UK.

ST PAUL'S CATHEDRAL

LOCATION:
Ludgate Hill,
London EC4M 8AD
TEL: 020 7236 4128
OPENING TIMES:
8.30–4 Mon–Sat
ADM: Cathedral only:
Adult £4, Child £2,
Conc's £3.50;
Charge for Galleries
Adult £3.50, Child
£1.50, Conc's £3

S T PAUL'S CATHEDRAL is one of London's greatest landmarks, an icon of the city itself, as familiar as Tower Bridge or Big Ben. Prior to the creation of Sir Christopher Wren's masterpiece, the site was occupied by a Gothic cathedral topped with a massive 500-ft spire. It burned down in the Great Fire of London with only a single statue of John Donne surviving. Wren's plans for a replacement cathedral initially met with considerable resistance. Intriguingly, it was the notion of a dome which particularly aroused

GETTING THERE:
Underground:
St Paul's,
Mansion House
Train:
City Thameslink
Bus: 4, 8, 11, 15, 17,
23, 25, 26, 56, 76,
172, 242, 501, 521
FACILITIES: Cathedral
shop, guided tours
available
DISABLED: No wheelchair access to
Galleries, access all
other areas
WEBSITE: www.
stpauls.london.
anglican.org

the Church authorities' hostility – "too Popish". Twice Sir Christopher submitted plans for a domed cathedral and twice they were rejected. Wren, convinced of the merits of a dome, persevered and was rewarded with a warrant of approval from the King allowing him to overule the church's objections. Nonetheless, the construction of the cathedral was carried out in as secret a manner as possible, with whole sections under wraps, to prevent further interference.

Time has proved the worth of Wren's vision. Interior highlights include the Whispering Gallery, 100ft up (so named because it is possible to whisper something on one side and have it heard on the other, 107ft away) and the beautiful carved choir stalls of Grinling Gibbons. There are fantastic views across the City of London from the Golden Gallery, 365ft up, just below the cathedral's topmost ball and cross.

STONEHENGE

LOCATION: Salisbury Plain, Wiltshire
TEL: 01980 624 715
OPENING TIMES: Daily; 16 Mar–31 May: 9.30–6, 1 Jun–31 Aug: 9–7, 1 Sep–15 Oct: 9.30–6, 16 Oct–15 Mar: 9.30–4
ADM: Adult £4, Child £2, Family £10, Conc's £3
GETTING THERE: Road: 2 miles west of Amesbury on the junction of the A303 & A344/A360 Train: Salisbury station (9.5miles) Bus: Call 01722 336 855 for details
FACILITIES: Parking available, gift shop, refreshments
DISABLED: Wheelchair access
WEBSITE: www.english-heritage.org.uk

As one of the world's most famous prehistoric monuments, Stonehenge has been much studied and yet is still only partially understood. What was the precise purpose of the stones? The significance of their astronomical alignments? The reason why the great blocks had to be transported all the way from south Wales? There are many questions still unanswered.

In the 1960s, the henge was adopted by many as a symbol of peace and renewal. However, clues hinting at a more grisly purpose have been found at nearby Wood Henge, a similar, albeit organic, monument where, in the centre of a circle of wooden posts, archaeologists have found the remains of a little girl axed to death as part of an ancient ceremony. It should be remembered that when they were first erected, sometime between 3000 and 1600 BC, the stones would have stood, not as they do now in splendid isolation, but rather as part of an extensive network of similar ceremonial monuments.

What isn't in doubt is the skill of the builders, who managed not only to transport the huge stones vast distances, but also, working with only very basic tools, erected and connected them using mortice and tenon and tongue and groove joints. Their expertise is evident in the fact that, 4000 years after they finished the job, around half of the structure is still standing.

STRATHCLYDE COUNTRY PARK

LOCATION:
Hamilton Road,
Motherwell ML1 3EA
TEL: 01698 266 155
OPENING TIMES:
Park, 9.30–dusk;
M&D's Theme Park,
call 01698 333 777
for details
ADM: Entry to the
park is free. M&D's
Theme Park is also
free entry, unlimited
rides pass Adult
£9.95, Child £6.75,
Family £30, individual
rides from 50p
GETTING THERE:
Road: From South:
M74 J5 or 6, from
North & West: M8,
M74, J5 or 6, from
East: M8, A725
Train: Nearest
station is Motherwell
FACILITIES:
Free car parking,
on-site Holiday Inn,
picnic sites, cafés,
restaurants, water
sports centre,
mountain bike hire,
pub, caravan &
camping site, guided
walks
DISABLED:
Wheelchair access
to theme park

SET IN THE industrial heart of Scotland, these 1,100 acres of mature woodland, rough wetland, wildlife refuges and neat open parkland constitute Britain's most popular country park. Over 4 million people visit the area each year to fish, go horse-riding or just sit and enjoy the spectacular rolling views. The focal point of the park is its loch, a great stretch of water home to cormorants, coots, mute swans and black swans as well as otters, water voles and even the odd osprey. Should you feel inspired to examine the wildlife more closely, you can hire rowing boats and canoes from the Watersports Centre. Fishing permits are also available; the loch is well stocked with bream, roach, carp and tench.

Other activities catered for within the confines of the park includes horse-riding – there are seven miles of bridle paths – and mountain biking.

A less strenuous alternative might involve a leisurely stroll through some of the park's 250 acres of mixed deciduous woodland, passing through the remains of a Roman fort and bathhouse on the way, before finishing up in the excellent loch-side restaurant.

As the sun sets, bathing the tree tops in a soft golden light, it's time to break the tranquillity and take a trip on the Tornado, Scotland's largest rollercoaster in M&D's, the park's very own themepark.

TATE BRITAIN

LOCATION: Millbank, London SW1P 4RG
TEL: 020 7887 8008
OPENING TIMES: 10–5.50 daily
ADM: Free, charges apply for some temporary exhibitions
GETTING THERE: Underground: Pimlico, Vauxhall
Train: Vauxhall
Bus: 2, 3, 36, 77A, 88, 159, 185, 507, C10
FACILITIES: Restaurant, café, shop
DISABLED: Wheelchair access, disabled parking spaces in the Clore car park can be booked on 020 7887 8813/4
WEBSITE: www.tate.org.uk

Originally intended as a showcase for British art when founded in 1897, Sir Henry Tate's gallery gradually lost sight of this vision over the course of the next century. In fact, by the early 90s, it had built up such a large collection of international art that the amount of space being given over to domestic product was continually being reduced. Something needed to be done. That something took the shape of a disused powerstation on Bankside which was transformed in the late 90s into a new Tate Gallery of Modern Art (see p.84). The old Tate, meanwhile, was reborn as Tate Britain, a gallery devoted entirely to British art. That interest in British art still exists is shown by the public's attendance of, and the press interest in, the Turner Prize for the best new British art, which is showcased here each year.

The revamped Tate has taken the unusual step of organising its collection thematically rather than chronologically, so you'll often see works by Renaissance portrait painters hanging alongside the latest shock-tactic conceptualism. All the greats of British art from 1500 to the present day are represented: from Constable, Gainsborough and Hogarth through Epstein, Spencer and Stubbs to Hockney, Moore and Hirst. Sir Henry would have been very happy. A century after its founding, it seems the gallery that bears his name is finally what he intended it to be.

TATE MODERN

LOCATION:
Bankside,
London SE1 9TG
TEL: 020 7887 8000
INFOLINE:
020 7887 8008
OPENING TIMES:
10–6 Sun–Thur,
10–10 Fri & Sat
ADM: Free
Getting There:

OPENED BY THE Queen to much fanfare in the early 1960s, by the early '90s Bankside Power Station was derelict and had been earmarked for demolition.

Coincidentally, the Tate Gallery was at this time looking for new premises in which to expand. Its collection had grown to such a size that thousands of works stayed permanently in storage. After toying with the idea of building a new purpose-built gallery, the Tate's board realised that the decaying power

Underground:
Southwark,
Blackfriars, London
Bridge
Bus: 45, 63, 100,
381, 344
Ferry: There's a ferry
service from
Embankment and
Festival Piers to
Bankside
Facilities: Café,
espresso bar,
licensed restaurant,
souvenier shop
Disabled: Wheelchair
access (entry via
North Entrance),
adapted toilets, nine
disabled parking
spaces call 020 7887
8888
Website:
www.tate.org.uk

station was, in fact, the answer to their prayers – a huge space that could be transformed into a gallery devoted entirely to Modern art.. The Swiss architects Herzog & de Meuron were entrusted with the task of turning this factory of electricity into the capital's latest showpiece art space. They took an evolutionary approach to the project, keeping the outer brick shell and central chimney intact while transforming the interior into a series of huge galleries, bathed in light streaming through a new 8.5 acre glass roof that spans the entire length of the structure. Universally acclaimed upon opening in the summer of 2000, it was declared a fitting rival to the Guggenheims and Pompidous of the world.

The gallery is split into three enormous levels where fine art, architecture, design, film and the decorative arts all have their own dedicated sections and holds works by such illustrious names as Dali, Matisse, Picasso, Warhol and Gilbert & George.

Once all its teething problems are sorted out, you will be able to arrive at Tate Modern from the north bank of the Thames across the new Millennium Bridge.

THORPE PARK

LOCATION: Staines Road, Chertsey, Surrey KT16 8PN

TEL: 01932 562 633

OPENING TIMES: Mar–Oct, times vary but usually opens at 9.30 or 10am and closes between 5pm and 7.30pm

ADM: Adult £16.50, Child £13, Under 1m free, Conc's £13, Disabled Adult £13, Disabled Child £10

ALL THEME PARKS need a showpiece ride, a glittering piece of terror-inducing hardware to set against the competition. Thorpe Park's champion is the bizarrely titled "X:/ No Way Out", which, although not the first roller-coaster to operate in pitch darkness, is certainly the first to force its passengers to travel at speeds of around 65 mph in the dark ... backwards.

This concession to modern super-thrill-seeking trends aside, most of the attractions at Thorpe Park have clearly been designed to cater for families rather than adrenalin junkies. Children are particularly well provided for, with various cutesily–named theme areas such as

GETTING THERE:
Road: M25 J11 or 13 (no access from J12), A320
Train: Chertsey station

FACILITIES:
Parking, various fast food outlets, gift shop, baby changing facilities

DISABLED:
Wheelchair access, adapted toilets

WEBSITE: www. thorpepark.co.uk

Mrs Hippo's Jungle Safari and Mr Monkey's Banana Ride, as well as Model World, which features miniature versions of the Eiffel Tower, the Pyramids and Stonehenge. They can also take a boat ride to the Thorpe Farm to bond with the resident goats, sheep and rabbits. Swimwear is a must, however, unless you want to return home with a car full of bedraggled children; there are more water-themed attractions here than at most parks, including the tallest log flume in the country; Thunder River, an ersatz white-water rafting adventure; and several pools and water chutes.

THE TOWER OF LONDON

LOCATION: Tower Hill, London EC3N 4AB

TEL: 020 7709 0765

OPENING TIMES:
Mar–Oct: 9–5
Mon–Sat, 10–5 Sun;
Nov–Feb: 9–4
Tue–Sat, 10–4
Sun–Mon

ADM: Adult £10.50, Child £6.90, Family £31, Conc's £7.90

GETTING THERE:
Underground:
Tower Hill
Bus: 15, 25, 42, 78, 100, D1

FACILITIES:
Car park, 4 shops, restaurant, coffee stall

DISABLED: Very limited wheelchair access, call 020 7403 1115 for access guide

WEBSITE: www.tower-of-london.com

KEEPING GUARD OVER Tower Bridge, this is one of the best-preserved medieval castles in the world. Built during the reign of William I, it has been used in its time as a stronghold for fugitive princes, as a jail for traitors and as the setting for some of British history's most notorious executions. Lady Jane Grey, Anne Boleyn and Walter Raleigh all ate their final meals here.

Today, the Tower's principal purpose is somewhat less dramatic. It is a Royal Museum dedicated to the preservation of all things monarchical. The Crown Jewels are here, as are various suits of armour including Henry VIII's bespoke model. The continued presence of the Tower's resident raven population is supposedly a prerequisite for the continued survival of the monarchy.

The Tower, previously rather hard on the legs, has in recent years become more user–friendly: there is a moving walkway to take you past the Crown Jewels, and the Tower Hill Pageant is a sort of underground ghost train ride past tableaux of famous historical episodes, with regular battle re-enactments by members of the English Civil War Society. And, of course, there are always the Yeoman Guards, or Beefeaters, to guide you around the principal sights.

THE VICTORIA & ALBERT MUSEUM

LOCATION:
Cromwell Road,
London SW7 2RL
TEL: 020 7938 8500
OPENING TIMES:
Mon 12–5.50,
Tue–Sun 10–5.50,
Wed Late View
6.30–9.30 (seasonal)
ADM: Adult £5, Child,
Disabled and their
Helpers free, Conc's
£3; free entry after
4.30pm
GETTING THERE:
Underground:
South Kensington
Bus: C1, 14 and 74
FACILITIES:
Licensed restaurant,
gift/book shops
DISABLED:
Wheelchair access
to most of the
museum. Use
Exhibition Road
entrance or call
020 7938 8638 to
book an escort in
advance
WEBSITE: www.
vam.ac.uk

PERHAPS THE V&S's most impressive feature is the sheer scope of its collection. These seven miles of galleries are stuffed to bursting with accumulated treasures: silverware, suits of armour, tapestries, paintings, sculptures, plaster casts, shoes, wallpaper – almost anything, in fact, which could possibly be categorised under the heading Art and Design. The variety is quite mind-boggling: there's a wonderful dress gallery where you can trace the evolution of fashion from the 17th century to the present day, from corsets, bodices and other forms of elaborate bondage to flapper dresses, miniskirts and

stilettos; a gallery devoted to William Morris; an Oriental and an Indian art section; a medieval tapestry section; a collection of Raphael cartoons; a gallery of 20th century design; the greatest collection of Renaissance sculpture outside Italy; and the greatest collection of Constables in the world. The Plaster Cast Room perhaps best encapsulates the essence of this temple of artifice and decoration – it is both the most impressive gallery in the museum and the one place without a single original artifact. Huge plaster cast models of the world's great sculptures, from Trajan's column (in two pieces) through Ghiberti's Gates of Paradise to Michelangelo's David, are on display in a vast hall.

PLans for the new 'Spiral' extension – conceived as an ivory-tiled 'explosion' against the traditional Victorian facade – are currently on hold.

WARWICK CASTLE

LOCATION: Warwick, Warwickshire CV34 4QU
TEL: 01926 495 421
OPENING TIMES:
Apr–Oct: 10–6 daily,
Nov–Mar: 10–5 daily
ADM: Adult £9.25,
Child £5.60, Under
4's free, Family £26,
Conc's £6.65
GETTING THERE:
Road: M40 J15
Train: Warwick
station

Warwick is one of the oldest and most evocative castles in England. Most of the present structure was built in the 14th and 15th centuries, although parts date back to the 10th century when it was home to Ethelfleda, daughter of Alfred the Great. In the Middle Ages the castle provided the back-drop for some of England's greatest intrigues and scandals. In the 14th century it was owned by Richard Neville, the Earl of Warwick, known as "The Kingmaker", the man who deposed both Henry VI and Edward IV. The Kingmaker exhibition in the castle's undercroft is an atmospheric tableau which aims, with the help of some suitably spooky

FACILITIES:
Free car park, 2
restaurants, café,
gift shop
DISABLED:
Wheelchair access
to ground floor only,
adapted toilets,
disabled parking
WEBSITE: www.
warwick-castle.uk

lighting and sound effects, to bring to life the preparations for the Earl's final battle. Visitors to the castle are also told the tale of Fulke Greville, a private landowner who con-verted the castle into a private mansion at the beginning of the 17th century and was brutally murdered by his manservant in 1628.

In the armoury you can try on medieval helmets and chain mail and practise a few thrusts and parries with a medieval sword.

The magnificent grounds were laid out in the 18th century by Lancelot "Capability" Brown and in summer play host to re-enact-ments of jousts and knights' combat.

WESTMINSTER ABBEY

LOCATION:
Parliament Square,
London SW1P 3PA
TEL: 020 7222 7110
OPENING TIMES:
9–4.45 Mon–Fri,
9–2.45pm Sat
ADM: Adult £5,
Child £2, Family £10,
Conc's £3
GETTING THERE:
Underground:
Westminster station
Bus: 3, 11, 12, 24,
53, 88, 109, 159,
X53, 211
FACILITIES:
Museum,
brass-rubbing
centre, audio tour,
book and souvenir
shop
DISABLED:
Wheelchair access
WEBSITE: www.
westminster-abbey.
org

WESTMINSTER ABBEY HAS, for a thousand years, been the focal point of England's royal, political and cultural life, the epicentre of Englishness, where every king and queen is crowned and buried, where every great statesman has a memorial plaque and where every great scientist, artist and writer is remembered. In recent decades, views of the abbey have been beamed around the world at times of great national significance. Two of the most-watched TV events in history, the coronation of Elizabeth II and the funeral of Princess Diana, took place here, when the huge vaulted interior became the image of England for the whole world.

The construction of the abbey required an effort of suitably regal proportions. Begun in the 13th century by Henry III, the nave wasn't finished until 1532 whilst the towers were only added in 1745. In recent years the similarly mammoth task of cleaning the exterior was completed, the grime and grit of centuries stripped away to reveal the beautiful sandy–coloured stone beneath – regular hawk patrols are in operation to stop nesting pigeons from restarting the deterioration process.

Interior highlights include the nave which, at 103ft, is the tallest in England, Statesman's Aisle, which features memorials to Palmerstone, Gladstone and Disraeli, and Poet's Corner where Dryden, Sheriden and Tennyson are buired and Shakespeare and Blake memorialised

WHIPSNADE WILD ANIMAL PARK

LOCATION:
Dunstable,
Bedfordshire LU6 2LF
TEL: 0990 200 123
OPENING TIMES:
10–4 daily
ADM: Adult £9.50,
Child £7, Conc's £7,
Disabled/Helper free
GETTING THERE:
Road: 20 mins
from M25 J21;
signposted from M1
J9 & 12. Just "follow
the elephants"
Train:
Luton and Hemel
Hempstead stations
Bus: Shires Services
from Luton and
Dunstable, call
0345 788 788, Green
Line buses from
London Victoria
(summer only), call
020 8688 7261
FACILITIES:
Gift/book shops,
cafés around park,
free bus around park
DISABLED:
Wheelchair access
to most of the park,
wheelchair hire
available
WEBSITE: www.
york.biosis.org/
zrdocs/zsl.htm

THE OPENING OF Whipsnade Wild Animal Park in 1931 was a landmark event in the history of wildlife conservation. It was Britain's first "open" wildlife park, the first to house its animals in large open paddocks (rather than cages) designed to mimic as closely as possible the animals natural environments. Today, spread over 6,000 acres of Bedfordshire countryside, Whipsnade is home to over 2,500 animals ranging from elephants, giraffes and rhinos to penguins, sea lions and chimps. Most inhabit large fenced enclosures, although there are also some "free" areas where peacocks, deer and wallabies can roam more or less at will. Staring benignly down upon the park is the famous Whipsnade lion, a 460ft-wide chalk picture cut into the Chiltern hillside in 1932.

Visitors to the park can choose to explore its attractions in one of four ways: by car, following the marked one-way route; by open-top tour bus; aboard the park's steam railway, which gently chugs its way around two miles of track; or even, in the free areas, on foot.

Not all of the park's residents live outdoors. Displayed in the Discovery Centre, in a series of controlled environments, are animals from some of the world's most inhospitable regions. Many of the reptiles here have been bequeathed to the park by Her Majesty's Customs officials, having been seized from people attempting to smuggle them into the country. For younger visitors there are daily demonstrations of bird handling and talks on the animals.

WINDERMERE LAKE CRUISES

LOCATION:
Launches: Bowness on Windermere, Cumbria LA23 3HQ. Steamers: Lakeside, Newby Bridge, Ulverston, Cumbria LA12 8AS

TEL: Launches 01539 531 188. Steamers 01539 443 360

OPENING TIMES: Open most of the year; earliest departures 9.05, latest 6.35

ADM: Two fare brackets available: boat only and boat & train/aquarium. Boat only returns Adult £5.50, Child £2.75. Boat & train/aquarium Adult £8.35, Child £4.25. Freedom of the Lake ticket Adult £9, Child £4.50, Family £24.50. Half-lake cruise ticket Adult £5.70, Child £2.85. Under 5's and 'well-behaved dogs' travel free

GETTING THERE:
Road: M6 J36, A590 Newby Bridge Road Train: Windermere, Oxenholme stations

FACILITIES: 300 parking spaces, coach parking, restaurants, cafés, licensed bars on boats. Gift shops on some steamers

DISABLED: Steamers suitable for wheelchair users but toilet facilities only accessed by stairs. Adapted toilets at Lakeside & Ambleside

WEBSITE: www. marketsite.co.uk/ lakes

IMAGINE YOURSELF LEANING against the rail of a classic 1930's steamer, glass of wine in hand, gazing out at some of England's most beautiful scenery as the sun begins to dip below the snowy mountain-peaked horizon. This, or something very like it, is what Windermere Lake Cruises hopes to offer. It's by far the most popular boating excursion in Britain, probably because of the great variety of cruises on offer. You can take a full three-hour jaunt around England's largest lake, all 21 miles of it, a half–length version (1¹/₂ hours) or opt for one of their wide variety of themed cruises. There's an island cruise, a wine cruise, a lunch cruise (which stops off at some of the elegant waterfront hotel restaurants), an evening buffet cruise, and even a submarine dive to the lake's ship-wreck-laden bottom.

A "Freedom of the Lakes" pass provides 24 hours unlimited travel on all the company's boats – there are launches as well as steamers allowing you to stop off at whichever of the lakeside attractions take your fancy. You can choose from the Windermere Steamboat Museum, the Beatrix Potter museum, the Lake District National Park Visitor Centre with its 30 acres of terraced gardens, or the Aquarium of the lakes, home to the largest collection of freshwater fish in England. You might even like to recreate a day-trip from yesteryear with a steam cruise to Lakeside and then a jaunty ride along the Old Furness Steam Railway Line through the Lake District's beautiful poet-inspiring countryside.

WINDSOR CASTLE

LOCATION:
Windsor, Berkshire
SL4 1NJ
TEL: 01753 868286
020 7839 1377,
Infoline
01753 831118
OPENING TIMES:
Mar–Oct: 10–5.30
(last admissions
5pm), Nov–Feb: 10–4
(last admissions
3pm)
ADM: Mon–Sat: Adult
£10, Child £5, Conc's
£7.50; Sun: Adult
£8.50, Child £4,
Conc's £6.50
GETTING THERE:
Road: M4 exit 6;
M3 exit 3
Train: London
Waterloo direct to
Windsor (every
30mins Mon–Fri).
London Paddington
via Slough (every
30mins Mon–Sun)
Coach: Victoria
coach station at
regular intervals
throughout day,
call 020 8668 7261
for details
FACILITIES: Coach
parking available
10 mins from castle
DISABLED:
Wheelchair access
to most areas of
castle
WEBSITE: www.
royal.gov.uk

THIS SPLENDID CONCOCTION of towers, ramparts and pinnacles is today the official residence of the Queen and the setting for innumerable state banquets and functions. The first wooden castle, built by William the Conqueror some 900 years ago to protect the western approach to the capital, was replaced with a stone version by Henry II 100 years later. A survivor from this time is the famous Round Tower, from the top of which, on a clear day, you can see no less than 12

counties. Later architectural highlights include St George's Chapel, founded in 1475 by Edward IV and finished by Henry VIII, with its amazing fan-vaulted ceiling, and the Queen Mary Doll's House, built by Edward Lutyens in the 1920s with perfectly scaled furniture and decorations.

In 1992, the State Apartments were ravaged by fire although, following £37 million worth of restoration work, you would be hard-pressed to tell. They are today as opulent as they ever were, and decorated with hundreds of priceless paintings from the royal collection, including Van Eycks and Rembrandts, as well as porcelain, armour, fine furniture and the carvings of Grinling Gibbons.

WISLEY GARDENS

LOCATION: Wisley, Woking, Surrey GU23 6QB
TEL: 01483 224 234
OPENING TIMES: 10–sunset Mon–Fri, 9–sunset Sat–Sun. Members only on Sun
ADM: Adult £5, Child £2, under 6's free, disabled/helpers free
GETTING THERE: Road: M25 Exit 10; follow brown tourist signs with flower symbol
Train: West Byfleet station 3 miles away; Woking station 5 miles away.
Bus: Call Guildford bus station for details 01483 572 137
FACILITIES: Free parking, restaurant, café, plant centre, book & gift shop
DISABLED: Free map showing best route around garden for wheelchair users. Shop, café & plant centre accessible. Adapted toilets
WEBSITE: www.rhs.org.uk

Set up by the Royal Horticultural Association in 1904, Wisley has become, over the course of the century, one of the country's best loved gardens. Although most people come to enjoy the beautiful planted borders, delightful rose gardens and glass houses, there is a more prosaic side to Wisley. It is also a valuable and well respected agricultural institute where cultivation techniques such as composting and pleaching are tried and tested and experimental model gardens are grown. The Gardens' Temperate Glass House was re-landscaped in the summer of 1998 and now contains a waterfall and pool. Elsewhere in this 240 acre site, you can find a traditional country garden, a farm, an orchard, a recreated alpine meadow, some delightful woodland and the new Garden of the Senses where a major collection of Bonsai is displayed. There's something to see all year round although the gardens are definitely at their best on a hot summer's day when the magnificent flower beds are in full bloom. Every August there is a popular flower show and a Family Fortnight when children's activities and entertainers are laid on. Living souvenirs can be picked up from the nursery.

WORLD NAVAL BASE, CHATHAM

LOCATION:
Chatham,
Kent ME4 4TZ
TEL: 01634 823 800
OPENING TIMES:
Apr–Oct: 10–6 daily,
Feb–Mar & Nov:
10–4 Wed, Sat & Sun
ADM:
Adult £8.50, Child
£5.50, Family £22.50
GETTING THERE:
Road: M2 J1 or J3,
M20 (J6)
Train: Chatham
FACILITIES:
On-site parking,
café, licensed
restaurant, gift shop
DISABLED:
Wheelchair access
WEBSITE: www.
worldnavalbase.
org.uk

Here, at these 400-year-old docks, you can find out about the quite fearsome logistics involved in building and maintaining a naval fleet. Shipbuilding, by its very nature, requires a lot of space, and this 80-acre site on the banks of the River Medway will take a lot of exploring with its vast, cavernous shipbuilding sheds and warehouses. In particular, check out the Rope-Making Room – officially, the largest room in the country – where great, thick quarter-mile long ropes are laid out on the floor and regular demonstrations of rope making are held.

At the "Wooden Walls" exhibition, you can see a series of waxwork animatronic tableaux designed to illustrate the construction of an 18th century warship. There are 15 historic lifeboats to explore – always a hit with kids who can run over the decks, pop their head through the portholes and sit in the captain's chair pretending to steer the ship – as well as an exhibition showing the importance of beer to the navy (it's been something of a love affair). The undoubted highlight of the museum, however, is "Battle Ships!", a display of three very different fighting vessels: HMS Cavalier, Britain's last remaining WWII destroyer, HMS Ocelot, a 1960's spy submarine, and the Gannet, the last Victorian fighting sloop (a small, extremely manouverable sailing warship mounted with about 20 guns), all of which can be toured and explored in the company of a guide. When the weather is good, trips are offered from the pier aboard a dockyard-produced paddle steamer.

YORK MINSTER

LOCATION:
Deangate,
York YO1 2HG
Visitor's Department:
St William's College,
5 College Street,
York YO1 7JF
TEL: 01904 639 347
OPENING TIMES:
Summer: 7–8.30pm
daily; Winter: 7–6
daily. No sightseeing
permitted before
1pm on Sundays
ADM: Free,
donations welcome
GETTING THERE:
Road: From South
M18 J2, A1, A64,
follow signs to York.
From North A68, A1,
A59, follow signs to
York
Train: Served by
GNER, Regional
Railways, Virgin
Cross Country, North
Western
Coach: National
Express provides
regular services to
York from all major
cities in the UK
FACILITIES: Gift shop,
conference centre,
restaurant and
catering facilities
DISABLED:
Some areas not
accessible for
wheelchairs, various
facilities available for
the visually impaired
and hard of hearing
WEBSITE: www.
yorkminster.org

THE LARGEST GOTHIC cathedral in northern Europe, York Minster is a supreme example of English medieval architecture. Its builders took a long time making sure they got it just so – begun in 1220, it was finally completed 250 years later.

Despite a couple of inflammatory episodes – fires in 1829 and 1984, started respectively by an arsonist and a lightning bolt, destroyed much of the original roof – today York Minster contains more medieval glass than any other church in England; approximately half, in fact, of all the medieval glass known to exist. After the last fire the roof was rebuilt at a cost of £2 million using, where possible, the traditional methods and materials of medieval builders.

The inside of the Minster is dominated by the fantastic stained glass east window which tells the stories of Genesis and Revelations, the top and tail of the Bible, in 27 exquisitely rendered panels. Other highlights include the wonderfully ornate ceiling of the Chapter House and the choir screen decorated with sculptures of every king from William the Conqueror to Henry VI. You can also climb the tower for some fabulous views out over the city of York.

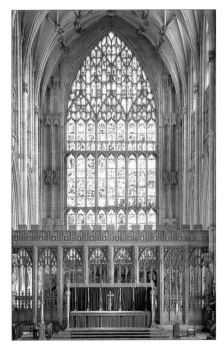

INDEX